John Francome retired from riding in April 1985 after becoming champion jockey for the seventh time. He and his wife Miriam, a fashion model, live at Lambourn in a house built by John. He now runs a stud farm and devotes his time to training horses. BORN LUCKY is his first book.

BORN LUCKY
an autobiography

JOHN FRANCOMBE

CORGI BOOKS

BORN LUCKY

A CORGI BOOK 0 552 13070 2

Originally published in Great Britain by Pelham Books Ltd.

PRINTING HISTORY

Pelham Books edition published 1985
Corgi edition published 1986

This book is set in 11/12pt Plantin.

Corgi Books are published by Transworld Publishers Ltd., 61–63 Uxbridge Road, Ealing, London W5 5SA, in Australia by Transworld Publishers (Aust.) Pty. Ltd., 15-23 Helles Avenue, Moorebank, NSW 2170, and in New Zealand by Transworld Publishers (N.Z.) Ltd., Cnr. Moselle and Waipareira Avenues, Henderson, Auckland.

Made and printed in Great Britain by the
Guernsey Press Co. Ltd., Guernsey, Channel Islands.

For my friends
An Autobiography is not the life story of a car!

INTRODUCTION

At fourteen Judith Johnson was quite simply the most beautiful creature I had ever seen. She had the face of an angel set on the body of a page three girl and moved on legs that seemed to end somewhere near her armpits. I fell in love with her the first time I saw her.

Unfortunately for me this schoolboy crush was carried on from afar. I wasn't quite twelve at the time.

The relevance of this little piece of imformation is that for two glorious years until she left to work in the sausage factory across the road, her games periods coincided with my English lessons and provided that I could get into the classroom quick enough to grab a desk by the window, I could spend a whole hour just gazing at her, which I did.

I've never regretted those many hours spent watching her run around in her gymslip and tee shirt but during the months I've struggled to write this book I've often wished that I'd missed any other lesson than English.

CHAPTER ONE

When things are going badly for you in racing the biggest mistake is to think that they can't get worse, as I found out in March, 1978. For almost six weeks I had been going through what I call a really character-forming period when everything went wrong to the point when I wouldn't have been confident of winning a walk over and was looking forward to a change of luck at Cheltenham. I never realised how serious a situation I'd got into until I opened the door to a dingy little interview room beneath the old grandstand and saw my governor, Fred Winter, sitting there together with the two chiefs of Racecourse Security and a female stenographer.

It was the second day of the 1978 Festival Meeting and the cold rain which had begun forty-eight hours earlier was continuing to fall in torrents from an almost black sky making racing unpleasant for both horses and jockeys and making the weighing room with its bright lights and friendly atmosphere an even more welcome sanctuary than usual.

I had already had one ride which had duly done its bit to continue my bad run and was sitting on my own in the corner, watching the valets struggling to clean the continual flow of muddy saddles. I was thanking my lucky stars that I wasn't one of them, when a tall official with a bowler hat, whose job it is to prevent anyone but jockeys and valets from entering the weighing room, came over and told me that Mr Anderson, the chief of Racecourse Security wanted to see me. Bob Anderson was a retired flying squad officer, who had taken over as head of Racecourse Security Services on his retirement from the force. Although I had never spoken to him before I had often seen him about at the races and knew who he was. On the wrong side of sixty he was a far cry from the image portrayed by Reagan on the television and looked more like Dixon of Dock Green with his dark blue suit and club tie, but whatever his appearance he was none the less very efficient at his job.

As I walked down the slope out of the weighing room to where he was standing I knew that it was going to be something to do with my association with John Banks. During our conversation he made me feel as though I was his best friend and when he told me to meet him in the room under the grandstand after the last race I just imagined that I was going to be given a quiet warning about John and told not to see him again, but the quiet warning turned out to be a police-type interrogation and Bob Anderson suddenly became a real hard copper. During the interrogation I was made to feel like a criminal and I don't mind admitting that for a few moments in there I was frightened. My heart began to pound so much that I thought they must all hear it and my legs felt as though I had just got off a horse after riding it non stop for a week. After the initial shock of having questions fired at me had passed, I pulled myself together. After all, I told myself, I hadn't murdered anyone, had I?

I had first met John completely by chance about two years earlier, when I found myself sitting next to him at the Stable Lad's Boxing Dinner and I had been fascinated by his story of how he had worked his way up from a Glasgow boy running factory workers' bets to being one of the wealthiest and most flamboyant bookmakers in the South of England. Apart from racing we shared a number of other interests including music and antiques. Although I should have been more aware of the possible connotations of our becoming friends we nonetheless did, and when I say became friends I mean he was a real friend, somebody who was always one of the few who rang up to see if I was all right after a fall and I was genuinely sorry later when our friendship had to end.

I don't know to this day how the rumours concerning us began but racecourses are notorious places for gossip. I suppose it only takes one person having lost his money on a horse I've ridden to see me with John for it all to begin, because the average punter will believe anything rather than admit that his judgement is wrong. To a certain extent I must take some of the blame myself because of some of the silly things I've said.

When you are riding successfully for a top stable such as Mr Winter's it is inevitable that it creates a certain amount of jealousy, especially when you are enjoying a particularly good run. If one of the fancied horses gets beaten you can be certain that a number of people will come up to you afterwards to commiserate when you know damned well they are actually delighted. Although these types are in a minority they still used to annoy me intensely and sometimes, to deny them their pleasure, I used to take them to one side and quietly tell them that the horse hadn't been trying and ask them whether or not it had looked bad, which in retrospect was stupid, but at the time it made me feel better.

I remember an old school teacher telling me that when he was in the army the general had sent a message back through the ranks of soldiers to 'send us reinforcements we are going to advance'. By the time it had reached those at the back it was 'lend us three-and-fourpence we are going to a dance'. Anyway I assume that by the time my known association with John had been around the racecourse a couple of times our friendship had turned into something far more sinister. Ironically it was my riding of a horse called Stopped that had brought things to a head and resulted in my being pulled in at Cheltenham.

There was no doubt that Stopped was a very good horse, but he was also a very hard puller and needed to be settled in the early stages of a race to prevent him running himself into the ground. Even if I do say it myself, it was largely due to my patience in teaching him to settle early in his career that made him the horse he was and to show the sort of form that explained his starting favourite for the 1978 Imperial Cup. Run at Sandown, the Imperial Cup is one of the most competitive handicaps of the year and because of the fast early pace I had no difficulty in settling him at the rear of the field. What did prove difficult was trying to weave my way through a pack of tired horses going around the last bend and ironically it was the Governor's other horse Acquaint, ridden by Bob Davies, that caused most of my problems. By the time I had extricated myself from the jam on the inside and had switched to the outside the race was already lost and we finished third to Winter Melody, ridden by Bill Smith. I understood the Stewards' reason for holding an enquiry to establish what had happened, but the fact that they only recorded my explanation, which really means that they don't believe what you have told them, annoyed me because the video recording of the race clearly showed that what I said had happened was true.

During the interview at Cheltenham I openly admitted to the RSS men that I had talked to John about the horses I had ridden because I had no idea it was contravening the rules of racing. Like ninety-nine per cent of jockeys I had never bothered to read them and despite telling them truthfully that I had never said anything to John that I wouldn't have repeated to the Governor or any of the owners, they decided to report the matter to Portman Square.

When finally I was allowed to leave, the Governor followed me outside. It was almost dark by this time and most of the racegoers had gone home. I didn't quite know what to say to him as we walked towards the weighing room and eventually I turned to him and said: 'Look, despite what has just gone on in there, I want you to know that I have never stopped a horse in my life.'

'Son,' he replied, 'if I thought for a moment that you had you wouldn't be standing there – you would be lying down!' With that he just walked on and never spoke another word about it.

If he had sacked me then and there nobody, including myself, would have been surprised but even the fact that he hadn't didn't stop me from wondering and worrying that maybe he might. I finally consoled myself with the fact that I had Miriam to go home to and that if the worst came to the worst, I could always earn a living helping my father.

Fortunately, Miriam is just like me and worries very little about anything, so after discussing the possible outcome we settled down as usual in front of the television. The only difference was that that evening the telephone rang continuously with press reporters wanting to know what was going on.

Not surprisingly, the interview had made headlines in most of the following days' racing pages, all of which were careful not to accuse either John or myself of having done anything illegal but nonetheless implying that we had. The atmosphere riding out at Uplands that morning was strained, to say the least. I had obviously been tried and found guilty by the lads before I had got to work, although none of them ever mentioned it. As for the Governor, it was impossible to detect whether or not he was cross because he is always grumpy in the mornings and seldom talks to anyone before 9.30, for which on that particular morning I was thankful.

Although the weather at Cheltenham on the first two days had been wet there was never any question of racing being called off and I couldn't believe my luck when I got in from riding out and heard that the final day, which included the Gold Cup, had been abandoned due to a freak snow storm, which had completely covered the course. Apart from the obvious relief of putting off for another day the time when I would have to face the crowd of 'we know what you've been doing people' it meant that the Gold Cup would be re-run the following month, when the ground was likely to be much firmer and much more to the liking of Midnight Court, who was my intended mount.

With no racing, the press were only too pleased to plaster the front of their papers with pictures of John and me. In the weeks between the interview at Cheltenham and the subsequent hearing at Portman Square, hardly a day went by without some reference to us, but the one that amused me the most came on 31 March in the *Sporting Life*. The headline read 'The Francome Banks Connection' above a picture of a car which I had owned. On either side were headshots of John and me chosen for their convict-like expressions. This dramatic headline did nothing but lead on to say how I had advertised my car for sale and then quite innocently sold it to John. Far from his giving me a vastly inflated price for it which they would have loved, because they could then have implied that I was being paid for information received, I actually sold it for £200 below book value.

Years of experience in training and riding horses during the British winter had taught the Governor never to rely on the weather and because of this he had taken the precaution of declaring Midnight Court for the valuable Aynsley China Chase at Chepstow just two days after the Gold Cup. As I had already won three races on him that season and he was my Gold Cup mount, I quite naturally expected to ride him and couldn't believe it when I was told that I had to go to Lingfield to ride a horse in a Novice Hurdle and that Graham Thorner had already been booked to ride Midnight Court.

I don't know to this day whether this was the Governor's way of punishing me for getting involved with John or whether he was thinking of sacking me but, as arguing with him is useless, I said nothing and went to Lingfield where I rode a winner. Faced with the sudden realisation that my job might hang on the outcome of Midnight Court's race I spent every available moment at Lingfield listening to the results at Chepstow and was depressed when I heard he had won easily. However the important thing was that he hadn't jumped very well for Graham, otherwise who knows what might have happened. Even though the Governor stood by me throughout the whole affair, I can't imagine that he never considered at some stage that perhaps I had been stopping horses, because my quiet style of riding often made it look as though I was. In later years people came to accept and appreciate the way I rode. I think Mr Winter appreciated it then and after Chepstow things went back to normal.

Luckily for me the revised date for the Gold Cup, following its abandonment, came just one week before the impending Jockey Club Enquiry which meant that barring accidents I would still be able to ride Midnight Court in it, no matter what the outcome.

Like a lot of horses at Uplands, Midnight Court had started his career in Ireland, trained by Tom Costello, before being bought by Dave Dick on behalf of George and Olive Jackson. Despite only winning one novice chase the previous season the Governor and I thought an awful lot of him as we kept running him against good horses and he improved with each race. The following season he had won six consecutive races before lining up for the Gold Cup on 13 April.

To be honest I don't remember much of the race other than the fact that Midnight Court won easily, but I do remember a tremendous feeling of relief as we passed the post and giving a Harvey Smith sign to the press box. At that moment I felt like Steve McQueen in *Papillion* when, at the end of the film, finally escaping on his coconut raft from Devil's Island, he shook his fist up towards heaven and shouted 'I'm still here, you bastard'. Despite being got at for almost a month I was still out there riding winners, and now I'd ridden a Gold Cup winner, just to really show them I wasn't beaten. It's the only line I have ever remembered from any film and in the years that followed it was often the first thing I shouted to the other jockeys when I returned to the Weighing Room following a lucky escape from a nasty fall.

When we returned to the winner's enclosure our reception was deafening. Pleased as I was for myself I was even more pleased for the Governor. This was his first Gold Cup winner, despite having saddled six previous favourites. Although I am not religious I couldn't help thinking that someone somewhere was rewarding him for his loyalty shown to me throughout the previous six weeks.

Being a virtual teetotaller I have never been much of a one

for celebrating so after dropping my parents off at Swindon, Miriam and I went home.

As with most private clubs the Jockey Club makes its own rules and then judges and penalises anyone who breaks them accordingly. Except for the fact that no press reporters are allowed, their enquiries are run on much the same lines as a normal court of law, with the Jockey Club Disciplinary Committee acting as judges, with solicitors to put their case and the defendants with solicitors to put theirs.

The enquiry took place on 30 April at the Jockey Club headquarters in Portman Square. My solicitor, Matthew McCloy, decided that it would be a good idea if both John and his solicitor met with us beforehand to discuss our plan of action and decided that the Churchill Hotel, which is just across the road would be a good place to meet. We prepared our case over breakfast and nearly fainted when we received the bill. It came to almost as much as the fine I got later. After recovering from that we walked across the square to number 42, where there was a large crowd of reporters and photographers waiting. Up until this point I really hadn't given too much thought as to the outcome, because in my own mind I knew I hadn't done anything wrong. When I saw the crowd standing there it suddenly struck me, however, that thirty people hadn't come to wait outside Portman Square, all day in the freezing cold, just to report that I had been given a good telling off.

The waiting area on the fourth floor where the enquiry was to be held is better than you would find in most executive offices, with thick red carpet and expensive oil paintings on the wall. Something happened just before we were called in which helped to relieve the tension. The lift in the Jockey Club is unlike any other lift I have used, with two sets of doors. The ones by which you enter it on the ground floor are opposite the ones by which you leave it on the fourth floor. As anyone who has ever used a lift knows the first thing you do when you get in is to turn around and face the door by which you have entered, ready to get out.

14

You then press the required level button by the side of the door and wait for them to close before looking up to the floor level indicator lights. Apart from letting you know when you have reached the appropriate floor, it usually saves you from having to talk to any strangers who may be travelling with you, then when the lift stops at your floor you wait for the doors to open, and get out. But what happens in Portman Square is that the lift stops and you hear the doors open behind you, which comes as a bit of a surprise, because from the inside the doors are almost invisible. What happened on this occasion, however, was that the man in the lift was on his own and, I imagine, partly deaf. As the doors opened we watched him standing inside with his back to us, looking alternately from the doors to the indicator light then, when nothing happened, he kicked the doors and rapped the level button with his umbrella before pressing the ground floor button to take him down again. After about a minute he reappeared, this time facing the right way, and went bright red as we all burst out laughing and gave him a slow handclap.

The enquiry began promptly at 10.30am and lasted for nine hours during which time the stewards and their solicitors asked John and me endless questions about races in which I had been beaten on favourites, trying to establish whether I had been stopping horses, for John's benefit. In the end they were convinced that I hadn't, although they found us both in breach of Rule 220(ii), which states that no-one shall do anything likely to cause serious damage to the interests of horseracing in Great Britain. This was because they said I had given confidential information concerning horses in training to John at his request. John was also found in breach of Rule 201(iv) in that he had 'surreptitiously obtained information about a trial' from me.

Because it had been established that I had broken a Jockey Club rule, I obviously expected some sort of penalty but the six week suspension and £750 fine was much more than I had bargained for. As for John, he was banned from every

15

racecourse in the country for three years and fined £2,500, which I thought was out of all proportion to the offence he had been found guilty of and, despite the High Court Appeal, the Jockey Club refused to reduce it, except to bring the fine within the maximum the Rules allowed the Stewards to impose at the time.

The first thing I did when I walked out of that room was to 'phone the governor, as promised. Then after being questioned by a mob of journalists who were still waiting outside, I drove home, relieved that it was all over.

For obvious reasons, John and I decided it would be best not to see each other afterwards, but I have heard from friends that during his ban, which was an enormous blow to him, he used the brains that had made him money bookmaking to do the same with American property. He has now returned to his old pitch on the rails and now that I have retired I am looking forward to renewing my friendship with him.

As for myself, the six weeks suspension followed by the summer break gave me just enough time to re-erect the industrial building which I had bought as an indoor school, but that's another story.

CHAPTER TWO

The only thing I was certain of when I left school was that I wanted to be independent and earn some money of my own. It was the summer of 1969 and my GCE results, or rather lack of them, had come as a big disappointment to my parents. After twelve years of education I had left Park Senior High School with only two pink pieces of paper as proof of my having been to school at all. One stated that I had obtained a low pass in metalwork and the other that I had managed an even lower one in geography, both of which were useless to a boy whose parents had plans for their son becoming a vet. I would dearly like to have done well at school for their sake as I appreciated how much they had sacrificed and how hard they had worked in order to give my sisters and me the opportunity they had missed but I am afraid that in those days lessons came a poor third behind ponies and football.

Life for me began in Swindon almost two years after my twin sisters, Jill and Norma. At that time we were living in a semi-detached council house but by the time I was given my first pony at the age of six, we had moved to a house of our own in a much nicer area. I am actually half-Welsh on my mother's side. She was born in Cardiff so any cunning in my blood should have come from her! (Only a Welshman could have conned Last Suspect into galloping around Aintree for $4\frac{1}{2}$ miles!) But she is the exception to the rule as it definitely comes from my father. My only connection with horses was a distant relative who went to prison for selling a blind horse to a woman as a hunter. It was only as I got older that I began to realise how hard my parents had worked. Dad was a fireman on the railway and used to cut people's hair and sweep

17

chimneys in his spare time to earn extra money while Mum kept chickens in the garden to help pay the rent. She even used to rear day-old chicks in the bedroom until the neighbours complained of the noise.

While our parents were struggling the twins and I were blissfully unaware of anything except how good life was. Within reason we were given most things that we wanted and everything we needed. No matter what we wanted to do they always encouraged and helped us and there was always good food for us to eat and warm clothes for us to wear. That last piece sounds a bit corny now but most of the kids I went to school with came from a rough area of Swindon, where even the Alsatians went round in pairs, and only ever had one cooked meal a week and only one set of clothes. We always seemed to have something to look forward to – like a weekend with Granny Francome where we were allowed to stay up late and watch TV or a week spent with my other grandparents in Cardiff with the occasional trip to the seaside at Barry Island.

It was at Barry Island that I first got bitten by the riding bug even though it was only a donkey, and when I went home I began helping the milkman with his round in return for a ride on his horse on the way home. Three months and lot of pestering later, my parents bought me my first pony. She had belonged to the milkman's daughter and was called Black Beauty although she was nothing like the magnificent creature I'd imagined Anna Sewell had written about. She was described as an ideal family pony which was accurate because her back was long enough to seat at least four children and frequently did for the first couple of months we had her.

Dad had just left the Great Western and had started out on his own doing odd jobs for people and the fact that for a year we had a pony, but no saddle, was an indication of how stretched my parents had been to afford the £50 for her.

My father is an amazing man inasmuch as absolutely nothing bothers him. No matter how many things go wrong

18

in a day he is never miserable and I have never heard him complain about anyone or anything. He was completely self taught as a builder, for years working on a trial and error basis and motivated by anything that somebody else said couldn't be done. His two favourite sayings are 'Make work a pleasure' and 'If all else fails read the instructions'. As his business grew and the houses we lived in changed for the better, so did the ponies and their accommodation and a railed paddock with a stable had replaced the allotment and old red railway wagon fenced with barbed wire. Beauty was followed by Tranzy who was followed by Ripper and then Willy Wagtail who was the prettiest pony I have ever seen. He was jet black with a silver mane and tail and silver spots on his quarters and was one of the quickest gymkhana ponies in England. We bought Willy from a farmer called John Wightman at Fairford whose son Peter I had become friends with at the local shows. Of the many happy memories I have as a child, I think the time spent on the farm with Peter were among the best.

During the winter every Saturday was spent hunting with the VWH. Peter's father would take us to the meet in his Land-Rover and trailer, then leave us to find our own way home. This was a far cry from the days of Beauty when our only form of horse transport was Dad's transit van with three scaffolding planks for a ramp. At the end of the day's hunting, we'd think nothing of hacking home twelve miles along the roads and disused railway lines, and we knew the country like the back of our hand. Our only concern was that we got home in time to do the ponies up and get indoors before Dr Who started at 5.15. I remember one day we had stayed out longer than we had wanted following a really good run and when we realised we wouldn't be home in time to watch the Daleks exterminating someone, we stood in somebody's garden holding the ponies while we watched their TV through the window.

Summers were spent at shows taking part in gymkhanas and the Prince Philip games, and when we weren't doing that, we were up at the farm fishing and shooting and rounding up his father's bullocks into an old air raid shelter so that we could tie a rope around them and ride them out like the cowboys in the rodeos. We also had an old motor bike to ride which we used to take out at night chasing hares. As it didn't have any lights I used to drive it and hold the torch while Peter sat on the back with a gun firing at anything that moved or was unfortunate enough to come near us. Although he had good ponies, Peter was never as keen a rider as I was, and when we grew out of them, and I went on to horses he gave up and he now helps his father manage the farm.

That first year of riding with no saddle was the best thing that could have happened to me as it taught me to grip properly with my legs which helped me to balance myself without the need to lean on the horse's mouth. Apart from Pony Club camp and half a dozen lessons with Mrs Sivewright at Cirencester and a couple later on with Dick Stillwell, I am self-taught and have learnt through experience and from watching the best people do whatever I was interested in whether it was show jumping or racing or anything else for that matter. Imitation may be the best form of flattery but it is also the best way for a beginner to learn.

Once I began show jumping I lost interest in gymkhanas altogether. Harvey Smith and David Broome were my heroes and it was them that I watched to learn. The turning point in my show jumping career, and without which I might have lost interest in riding altogether, came when my parents bought me a horse called Red Paul. He was a Grade 'A' and it was with him and on whom I represented Great Britain abroad in France and Switzerland where we won the European Championships. Competing with a better horse meant travelling further afield to more shows in order to qualify for different finals and, after a night spent sleeping in the car at Hickstead, Dad swapped the trailer for a horse box with living accommodation. To be fair it was Mum who usually accompanied me to the shows because Dad always seemed to be too busy but I think she enjoyed it as much as I did.

Although I wasn't quite sixteen I did most of the driving as my mother wasn't really strong enough and in two years we only got stopped once. It was on the way to Butlin's Show at Minehead and there was a traffic census in Frome. The policeman who stopped us asked me everything except whether I was old enough to drive before he let us go and the incident aged my mother about ten years! If I told my Dad I was going to rob a bank he wouldn't mind and would probably ask if he had anything I needed! But Mum is the complete opposite – she would walk back into town if she found a shop assistant had over-paid her. When Dad had a bad car accident during that summer and Mum was forced to stay at home to look after him, I used to go off to the shows with the horses on my own rather than miss them, which was crazy, but it was great for my confidence to know that they trusted me.

For some reason most people who have anything to do with horses of any description are very likeable and we made a lot of good friends while we were doing the show circuit. To give you an idea of how small the horse world is Fred Fox, who is now Mr Winter's blacksmith, used to work for Tom Brake when he was jumping Lizawake and spent most of his time at the shows in our horse box eating Mum's bacon sandwiches. Another person in racing now who started with show jumping is Derek Kent who went on to win two Colonial Cups with Grand Canyon. It was myself, Derek and two of his staff, Annie and Angela, who travelled the five ponies in the British Team out to Switzerland in 1970. Derek was then private trainer to Michael Hall-Hall who was another member of the team. Considering the time I spent away from school show jumping, it was a miracle I was even there for the exams, let alone that I passed any. But when I was there, I saw enough to appreciate the difference between life with money and life without; and if anyone ever tells me, it's tough at the top I always reply 'It's a bloody sight tougher at the bottom'.

Park Senior High was formerly a Grammar School in the middle of a housing estate in Swindon. Then the education system was changed to avoid children getting an inferiority complex by being sent to a secondary modern school after they failed their eleven plus. This was just as well for Chris Potter who sat in front of me in class because he had such an inferiority complex he nearly gave up rugby because, every time there was a scrum, he thought the other lads were talking about him! If we weren't the most academic bunch at school, we certainly knew what two and two added up to and how to get it. For most of them making money was a necessity but for me it was just a game. I loved doing it then and I love doing it now, not because I am greedy but because I enjoy the challenge of a deal. At school anything that made money was fair game whether it was legal or not. My business interests ranged from running the tuck shop to printing counterfeit lunch vouchers which I sold to a limited amount of pupils at half price.

Trevor Walters however had the best business in school. When the job of milk monitor became vacant he had somehow persuaded the form teacher that he should be the new replacement. Within a month he made an arrangement with the milkman whereby for 5/- a day he would take four gallons of milk less. The milkman then sold his surplus on the side while Trevor compensated the shortfall by diluting the milk with water while everyone was in assembly. Just as Stephen Smith-Eccles is now and Victor Soane was whilst I was an apprentice, Trevor was my best friend, but our friendship came to a strange end. For four years we were like brothers – we caught the same bus to school each day and did everything together from playing truant to painting white emulsion in stripes on the caretaker's cat. Then on the very last day of term after all the celebrating and well wishing was over, we sat in the classroom window of 4B and watched for the school bus to arrive. We reminisced about

22

the things we had done together over the years and how we had become such great friends after he had unhitched me from two of the pegs in the cloakroom. I had been left hanging from them on the collar of my blazer as a punishment for being caught by two sixth formers with my hand up their vending machine. I was replacing a plastic cup which I had pierced with my compass. It was just unfortunate that one of them had got the cup I had tampered with the day before and still had the coffee stains on his trousers to prove it. We also recalled how his turn as milk monitor had come to a premature end following an English lesson with Mr Hubbard who was also our form teacher. It was at the time of the new television commercial advertising tea bags and, during what was supposed to be a serious lesson on the origin of words and their spelling, Mr Hubbard had looked up and asked if anyone had any questions. Trevor put his hand up and with a really serious look said 'Yes, Sir, if Typhoo put tea in Britain who put the c--t in Scunthorpe?'

When the old yellow bus finally appeared there were scarves and satchels hanging out of every window belonging to children delighted to be leaving school or going home for the holidays. We were all still laughing and shouting when the bus stopped to drop me off at the lay-by just outside Swindon for the last time. As I got up and collected my stuff from the rack I said 'See you' to Trevor, as I always did and waved goodbye to everyone as the bus pulled away. That was the last time I ever saw him. It was just as though a big screen came down and someone said 'O.K. that's the end of Act I, school's over, and there will be a new cast for Act II.' We didn't even telephone one another.

CHAPTER THREE

Although I had been riding since I was six, I was never remotely interested in racing and, as a consequence, had never considered becoming a jockey for a career until I received my exam results. With the success I had achieved show jumping, the obvious thing for me to do when I left school was to carry on with that but I realised that there is an enormous difference between competing as a hobby, where if you covered your expenses it was a bonus, and actually trying to make a living from it. Also I was concerned with what the financial burden to my parents would have been. I knew they would willingly have supported me but I felt they had already done enough for me and to become a jockey suddenly seemed the natural solution.

Having made my mind up as to what to do it was pure chance that I ended up with one of the best trainers in England and, more importantly, one with whom I would be given a chance of making it as a jockey. I had no idea then that the majority of trainers had no intention of helping anyone else but themselves and apprentices were just a form of cheap labour. I had never heard of Fred Winter, but a friend of my father's had once done some work for him at Uplands and suggested that I went to see him. It is amazing to think that my career in racing was based on the advice of a carpenter who probably didn't know which end of the horse to feed but, as it turned out, was a good judge of character. The long and the short of it was that my father got in touch with the Governor and on 16 September 1969 we went for an interview.

I can remember that day as if it were yesterday not just because it was my first interview for a job but because of the impact the whole place had on me. I had never seen such a beautiful house and garden with its wonderful avenue of horse chestnuts leading down to it and the stable yard was immaculate. It was 5pm on a Saturday evening when I arrived with my parents. The head lad, Brian Delaney, was shovelling mash from a barrow into galvanised buckets as the lads ran back and forth feeding the horses. When we rang the door bell, Denise, the Governor's eldest daughter, answered the door and showed us into the office where the Governor was writing. I suppose it is because we got older together but I don't remember that he looked any different then than he does now with his weather beaten face and his combed-back hair. He was certainly just as neatly dressed with ruler straight creases in his trousers and highly polished shoes. After having been introduced I told him how much riding I had done. He stood me on a pair of bathroom scales and weighed me; I was 10 stone 4lb. I then asked him what my chances were of becoming a jockey. He paused for a moment before answering, during which time he took a good look at my father who weighed close to 14 stone. He then said that taking into account my weight for my age, the size of my hands and feet and the size of my father, he thought that I would probably become too heavy, but if I wanted to try I could start as an apprentice the following month.

With only two 'O' levels the world wasn't exactly my oyster and I accepted there and then, and so on Sunday 16 October 1969 I began a job which was to last for sixteen years, during which time there would be many ups and downs but, given my time again, I wouldn't change a thing.

For any parents too embarrassed to explain the facts of life to their son I can thoroughly recommend, as a suitable alternative, a short spell working in a racing yard. Other than horses, sex is the only topic of conversation discussed in any detail and any boy who still isn't quite sure what everything is for and what should go where after his first five days need only wait for the weekend when the lads' girlfriends arrive. He will then be able to watch quite openly any number of live demonstrations, which was exactly the scene when I walked into the hostel that Sunday evening.

The hostel at Uplands where I lived for my first two years in Lambourn is a long wooden building with a dining room cum TV room and kitchen at one end and three small bedrooms at the other where twelve of us slept in bunk beds. As a new boy I was given a lower bunk. Of the twelve beds, four were occupied by lads entertaining their girl friends, or at least I thought that they were their girl friends. One, I later discovered, was the wife of the local school teacher who was away organising a Duke of Edinburgh Award Scheme. It was just the sort of thing one expects to see in a comic blue movie but never imagines happens in real life. Trying to find your way around a new building while at the same time desperately trying to keep your eyes off the rocking beds and not be noticed is not easy and, as soon as I discovered where I was to sleep, I dumped my suitcase and bumped my way back to the other end of the hostel where I played darts and waited for someone to arrive. At six o'clock it was as though a silent bell had been rung, everyone from the bedrooms suddenly got ready to go to the pub and I was introduced to everyone. They were a tremendous bunch of lads at Uplands in those days, all intent on enjoying themselves. Each one had gone into racing with the intention of becoming a jockey but, from the twelve, only Vic Soane and Derek King had been given rides. Those who hadn't consisted of four apprentices, myself, Clive 'Digger' Rodway, Roy Woodward and Paddy O'Brien, all of us hoping to become jockeys, while the remainder had resigned themselves to the fact that they weren't good enough. As time went on they all left to take other jobs in racing. Peter Heaney, Corky Brown and Joe Tanner are now Head Lads. Joe is with me whilst Pete and Corky are with Nick Gaselee and Nicky Henderson respectively. Then there was Tich Bryan and Loppy Smailes who are now box drivers. Loppy lives in Lambourn and is married to my sister, Norma. Finally there was Mick Cullen, who is now the Governor's Travelling Head Lad and the only one of the original dozen still at Uplands.

To say that there wasn't room to swing a cat in the hostel is an understatement and from my bunk I could lean out and touch the bunks on the other side of the room. Clothes space consisted of seven inches in which to hang things on a twenty-eight inch rail and woe betide anyone who took eight inches. The only other space was an open shelf measuring thirty inches by twenty inches, where you had to keep everything else including your all important wash bag. I say all important because, in two years of living in the hostel, there was never the slightest worry that someone would steal any money from you, but dare to leave a bar of soap or shaving cream behind you in the bathroom for more than two seconds and that would be the last you saw of it.

I shared a room with Titch, Digger and Paddy. Titch had been at Uplands for three years and it was his job to make sure that the apprentices kept the hostel clean and tidy. Digger and Paddy had only started the week before me. Before you get the wrong idea, let me tell you that Digger earned his nickname from the love affair that his index finger had with his nose and not from a flair for gardening as I had originally thought.

At home, bedtime for me had usually been about nine thirty. In the hostel, nobody went to bed until the dot had appeared on the television screen, especially the apprentices, who were treated like fags at a public school, in as much that at any time of day or night or at least until the pubs had closed any of the older boys could send them to fetch whatever was needed. If anyone ever dared to say 'No', which they only did once, they were strung upside down naked in the shower while the older lads painted their private parts with hoof oil. This in itself wasn't so bad – it was the stiff brush they put it on with that hurt.

My first morning came as something of a shock. I had been used to my mother waking me up gently at about seven thirty with the offer of a cup of tea. At Uplands I was woken at six thirty by Brian Delaney barging his way through the hostel shaking the bunks and shouting 'Come on jockeys, get your hands off your cocks and pull on your socks'. Apparently he had been waking the lads up like this every morning since he had taken over the job as Head Lad from Tommy Deary and, as far as I know, still does the same to-day. Because of space shortage we had to take it in turns to get up and dressed, but there was no problem in the wash rooms. Only three of us ever washed before work. As for the lavatories, if the architect who designed the hostel had any idea of the quantity of beer a lad can drink in one evening, he would have realised that three urinals and one lavatory were nowhere near adequate to cope with twelve bursting bladders early in the morning. I won't go into the sordid de-tails but you can imagine what a mess three lads make when they are all trying to pee into a piece of china six inches wide at the same time, while their aim is being misguided by a fourth jostling desperately for non existent room. Nobody went for a pee without something on their feet.

My first morning was nearly my last. By eleven o'clock I had had two bollockings from the Head Lad for doing things I had been doing at home for years. The first came when I went to muck out my horse. After tying it up I decided to switch on my transistor radio which I had in my anorak pocket. The instant the music started the horse went berserk, knocked the radio out of my hand into the straw and pinned me up against the manger. It then tried to run backwards and as it did so slipped and was left hanging upside down from its chain, not moving; for a split second I thought I'd killed it, then thankfully the head collar snapped and it dropped to the floor. It then scrambled to its feet and began racing round and round the stable like a dog with worms. Between two of its laps I managed to dive into the corner, pick up the radio and get back before it came round again. The instant I turned the radio off it began to calm down, along with the other twenty-six horses which had been within ear shot, all of which had apparently been performing similar exercises to the music. Thankfully only four of them had broken their

28

head collars, but one had got loose onto the Governor's lawn which didn't go down too well, as it was his pride and joy. He had only just finished repairing it after fifteen of his next door neighbour's bullocks had got out one night after it had been raining and had left it looking like a ploughed field.

My second mistake came after breakfast when I went to tack up my horse and started putting its bridle on before I had even opened the door. I was talking to one of the other lads whilst adjusting the cheek pieces when Brian walked round the corner and pointed out at the top of his voice the stupidity and obvious danger to the horse of what I was doing. While I reckon that my first mistake was excusable, I knew that the second one wasn't and told myself that I had better start thinking a lot harder and take heed of the professional way things must be done when handling expensive animals belonging to other people. By the time I went home for the summer after my first season at Uplands, I had learnt more about the fitness, management and feeding of horses than I had in seven years of show jumping, and figured that if I was never given a ride in public, that time would not have been wasted. Obviously I learnt most from Brian, for whom I have always had a great deal of respect, and in sixteen years I have never come across a better Head Lad. Apart from being a first class stable man, he has a tremendous way with the lads, giving them just enough rope to enjoy themselves without losing any of his authority. Any lad found not pulling his weight or doing his job properly was given one warning and then told to leave. Having said all this I have to admit that for a time I hated the bastard, although I never let him know it. I don't know why, but for some reason he never seemed to like me, and if he had the chance to be awkward, he would. He loved to find me jobs to do after work, so that by the time I got into the hostel for supper it was invariably cold and someone had eaten my pudding. On my weekends off, when he knew I would be in a hurry to get on my scooter and go home, he'd wait until I and the other apprentices were leaving the yard after washing out the mash barrows and tidying up after the other lads, then he would call me back and say 'Sonny' (he called everyone excluding the Governor 'Sonny'). 'Sonny, go and feed that horse and donkey in the paddock.' The horse in question was an ex-racehorse called Robin Hill, who had been retired to the paddock along with a donkey for company. I then had to mix the mash, find a torch and trundle off into the freezing night to find these two ungrateful beasts, who made a point of standing in the furthest corner of the field. He used to watch to make sure that I just didn't tip their feed over the gate. As he was Head Lad, however and had the Governor's ear, I knew it wouldn't do any good to fall out with him and realised that in fact I had the opportunity to kill two birds with one stone.

For an ambitious sixteen-year old the path to becoming a jockey had started to look like being a very long one. I was the newest apprentice and as such was last in line of four lads waiting to be given the opportunity to ride schooling, which is the crucial stage in any budding jump jockey's career. This opportunity doesn't come very often when you already have three professional jockeys in the yard, and when it does, you have to make the most of it. If you do well you will be given the chance to school again the next time, but if you don't you will probably have to wait months before you are given another go. I decided that if I worked exceptionally hard I might be able to jump the queue a couple of places by wheedling my way into Brian's good books. From then on I made a point of being the first lad into the yard every morning so that I had time to get the Governor's and Brian's horses tacked up ready for exercise as well as my own. When we came in I tied my own horse up and threw a rug over him before running round to do the Governor's horse up after which I rushed back round to do my own. Doing this made me last in for breakfast, but I made sure that I was first out so I could do the same thing all over again second lot. In the yard I took charge of both saddle rooms and feed house and made certain that everything was kept cleaner and tidier than it had ever been before. I made sure that the dustbins were out on Wednesday and that there were always enough oats crushed and carrots chopped ready for feeding, then if I could make it, I tried to be first on the broom when it came to sweeping up at the end of the morning. By the time I'd finished there weren't many jobs left for the other apprentices and I was often accused, quite rightly, of creeping which didn't embarrass me in the slightest! My plan worked. Within three months of starting I was given my first ride schooling on an old horse called Kilkoran while two of the other apprentices, who had been in front of me in the queue, were still waiting.

I was in something of a panic that first morning when I walked into the tack room and saw that I was down on the board to ride schooling. To begin with I didn't have a whip because only the schooling jockeys had them so I had to cut a stick from the hedge. Secondly and much more of a problem was the fact that I didn't have a crash helmet. In those days helmets weren't compulsory and you were considered soft if you rode out with a hard hat. I remember the Governor telling me about when he turned up at Ron Smyth's yard for the first time, to school with a helmet under his arm. 'What's that?' asked Ron. 'My schooling helmet,' replied the Governor. 'Well you can put that back in the car, lad, we're not soft here and we don't use helmets.' The Governor said he must have been just as stupid as Ron because he did as he was told. With no helmet I had to make do with Roy's motor bike hat which I tied on with baler twine. The chin strap was missing. To say that I looked a mess was putting it mildly and it was a wonder that the Governor didn't send me home the moment I arrived on the gallops. That afternoon, when I'd finished work, I went straight down to the saddlers and bought myself all the proper equipment.

Appearances apart, my first morning's schooling went well. Mind you it should have done, Kilkoran had schooled so many times before that I needed to do little more than point him in the right direction. This was the first time I had

31

jumped anything in months and I had forgotten how much I enjoyed it. Over the years I went through intervals of being fed up with driving and dieting and just about every other part of a jockey's life you can think of, but I never lost my enthusiasm for schooling whether it was at Lambourn, where Eddie Fisher built the best fences in England, or in a field on someone's farm jumping forty-gallon drums. I suppose this was because it was the part of my job that I was best at and I took a real pride in it. By the time I took over from Richard Pitman as first jockey in 1975, the Governor was already leaving most of the schooling decisions to me. I took real pleasure in teaching the young horses to jump properly and, even if I do say it myself, excelled in knowing what to do if they didn't. With a young horse that doesn't want to jump it is important to know straight away whether it is because it is nervous and needs encouragement or whether it is taking the mickey and wants a good crack around the backside. If you make the wrong decision with a nervous horse, you can spoil it for a long time. The main point always to remember is that if a horse doesn't enjoy himself, he will never be very good at his job.

Schooling mornings in Lambourn early in the season when the ground is just beginning to soften are bedlam. There can be anything up to fifty horses waiting to be schooled and most of the trainers are corked ready to pop at any mistake made by anyone, except themselves. I think they must have their own little competition to see who can give the loudest bollocking but, since Jenny Pitman started training, they have only been competing for second place. On a still morning you can hear when something has gone wrong with one of her horses from over a mile away!

By far the largest number of bollockings is given to apprentices having their first ride schooling. Most have never jumped anything in their lives before and despite advice from me to go to a riding school and get some jumping instruction to give themselves a better chance, not one ever bothered.

Digger ruined any chance he ever had of becoming a jockey on just such an occasion but it wasn't only his inexperience at jumping that let him down. He had never ridden a horse at all when he went to Uplands and had gone into racing for no other reason other than he and his father were compulsive gamblers. Even after a year you still wouldn't have let him sit on your bike – let alone school a racehorse but school it he did, or at least he tried. It might not have been so bad if he had been on a horse of no consequence but he wasn't. Every now and again the Governor falls in love with one particular horse that has usually got lots of ability but which is mulish and he doesn't take kindly to anybody even suggesting that the animal might be ungenuine. After doing everything wrong bar falling off, Digger dismounted and told the Governor that Nantar, which was the horse he had just schooled, was so slow that it would be better suited between two shafts! That was one apprentice out of the way. Paddy had already delayed his chance of becoming a jockey a few weeks earlier when a horse called Gold Finder got down and rolled with him on the way home from the Gallops. Paddy had never seen a horse roll before and thought that the horse was dying. He shouted to the Governor, who was at the front of the string to come quickly which, unfortunately, for Paddy, he did. The Governor arrived just in time to hear the tree of a new saddle breaking.

I was a long way from being perfect myself but the errors I made weren't in my riding and instead of anger, my mistakes brought out the Governor's sarcasm. I remember on one occasion the Governor had ridden a horse up to the schooling ground and I was to drive up in the car and get on it up there. It was early on in my second season and unbeknown to me the hurdles had been moved from the top of the Gallops into a little hollow where the ground was slightly softer. Just as I arrived where I expected the hurdles to be, I saw the Governor and the horses that we were to school disappearing over the brow of the hill and assumed that on seeing that the hurdles weren't up, had decided to go

33

and gallop the horses instead. For about ten minutes I sat in the car listening to the radio waiting for them to come back so that I could ride the Governor's horse home. Then I got bored and thought that I would walk over and meet them. As I topped the brow of the hill and looked down to the Gallops below my heart stopped. About a quarter of a mile away I could see a line of hurdles and our horses waiting to school. I forgot about the car and ran as fast as I could down the hill through the waist-high barley to where they were. I arrived panting and began explaining to the Governor why I was so late. When I finished he said 'That's all right son, it's not your fault,' and I thought 'Thank God for that.' He said 'It's my fault – you're so fucking stupid I should have written your instructions down on a blackboard.'

When I was young and keen I'd school anything for anybody as long as it had four legs but as time went on and I became more established as a jockey, I grew less tolerant of trainers who expected me to school really bad jumpers. One morning after jumping a horse that had failed to take a leg off the ground at three consecutive fences I went back to the trainer and told him that the horse didn't feel right and that I thought there was something wrong with his back. 'He looks OK to me,' said the trainer 'just go and jump three more fences and see if he is any better next time'. 'If he looks OK to you,' I said 'then you ride him,' and with that I dismounted and handed him the reins. The trainer who had only the year before stopped riding as an amateur said, 'Don't be silly, John, I'm not going to school him.' 'Well, if he isn't safe enough for you to ride, he definitely isn't safe enough for me,' I said, and with that the horse was sent home. I never minded how long I spent teaching bad jumpers to be better but I drew the line at risking my neck on horses that were physically unsound.

If I worked hard in the yard to get rides, it was nothing compared to what I did out of hours in an effort to save enough money in order to exchange my scooter for a car. My time at school began to pay dividends. Regular jobs included changing all the sheets in the hostel for a shilling a bed every Monday because the other lads hated to change theirs, and washing both the Governor's and Brian's cars for 10/- a week.

My best job though was babysitting for Richard Pitman and Willie Robinson. To get paid for sitting down doing virtually nothing all night in a comfy chair with free access to the larder was my idea of heaven and I willingly gave up my nights out with the other lads when either of them asked me.

Once I got a few pounds up together I began lending the other lads money when they were short, which for some was about 3 o'clock on a Friday afternoon after they had lost their wages playing cards. The conditions were that they could borrow up to £20 each but had to pay it all back plus five per cent the following pay day. If they wanted to borrow another £20 then they could. I had a slight set back with this banking venture when I made the mistake of lending £10 to a lad from Dave Hanley's yard. He was a big rough looking lad from Glasgow and I should have known better than to lend him anything in the first place but felt that the time had come to expand my business out of the hostel. Anyway what happened was that when I went to collect my debt the following week he went for me with a carving knife and threatened to cut my ears off if I didn't go away. I think 'piss off' were the exact words he used. For the sake of a tenner I certainly wasn't going to risk losing the only things I had to keep my sun glasses on and did as I was told. From then on I was much more careful to whom I lent money.

One of my other ventures that I began later that failed was a car hire business but this was due to the fact that I couldn't afford a reliable car and had nothing to do with bad debts. I decided on this idea because I'd noticed that while most of the lads in the village could drive, hardly any could afford a car of their own.

The vehicle I had made the mistake of choosing was a light green Cortina and, as soon as I had insured it, I had advertising posters printed and pinned them up in all of the hostels around Lambourn and most of the pubs and shops as well. Although it was reliable enough on short journeys it never failed to break down at weekends and I spent three consecutive Saturday nights in different parts of the country repairing it while whoever had hired it continued their journey in my car. The final straw was when Brian's father-in-law Fred Hodges hired it to go to Cornwall for the week and the starter motor packed in when he got there. Because it was my weekend on (you get every other weekend off – if you call Sunday a weekend) I drove to Cornwall straight after work on the Saturday but it took me all Saturday night and most of Sunday to repair it and, as a consequence, I had to telephone the hostel and pay Clive to work for me. Having driven to Cornwall and spent most of Sunday under the bonnet of the car I didn't think that the weekend could get much worse. But as I was pulling away from a crossroads in Devizes the clutch packed up. That was the last straw. I decided the car hire business was definitely not for me. I pushed it into a nearby garage and then forked out £19 for a taxi back to Lambourn. The following morning I phoned the garage to explain what a broken down Cortina was doing on their forecourt and to see if they wanted to buy it from me. The price they offered virtually amounted to stealing but I'd had enough and accepted. I posted them the log book and about three weeks later they sent me my money.

As I still had one summer left in Young Riders' Competitions we had kept Red Paul throughout that winter at Richard Pitman's yard in Wanborough. This tiny little village is only seven miles from Lambourn and I used to drive over after work and put into practice everything that I was learning at Uplands and by the time the first big show came around at Amberley I had the fittest show jumper in England. That was the middle of April and although I was schooling regularly there was no question of getting a ride in public until the following season. The ground was drying up and the runners from Uplands were getting progressively fewer so I decided to leave early before the end of the season and have one last fling at showjumping.

The start of the show season is always good fun. It's the time when you meet all your friends from around the country whom you haven't seen since the end of the previous season, and there is always lots of news to talk about and plenty of good parties. This last season of show jumping was easily my best and after winning a Gold Medal in St Moritz with the Junior Team, I came back to Hickstead to win the Young Riders' Championship of Great Britain. Suddenly I started to have doubts about just how much I wanted to become a jockey and an offer from Harvey Smith to jump his second string of horses only helped to make my decision more difficult but in the end I decided that it would be a pity to waste a winter's hard work and so, after the Horse of the Year Show was over, and Red Paul had been sold to Debbie Johnsey I returned to Lambourn.

CHAPTER FOUR

In just over a year my weight had risen by 8lb to 10st 12lb and, when my first ride in public came along, on Multigrey at Worcester in December, I had 7lb to shed in less than four days. By running with a sweat suit on and not eating anything I managed to lose 4lb and relied on two laxative tablets the night before to lose the rest. The ones I took were disgusting and the size of disprins. To say the effect of taking them is unpleasant would be something of an understatement especially if they start taking effect as you are half way home from the Gallops on a horse that keeps jig-jogging! Carl Lewis wouldn't have beaten me from the stable to the lavatory in the hostel on that first morning but, after a while, I got it timed to perfection so that they worked just as I woke up. Even after spending most of breakfast time on the loo, I was still 2lb too heavy and had to borrow half a pee pill from Richard Pitman to get rid of the remaining weight. Richard regularly lost anything up to 10lb in a morning by taking just one and the half I took worked so well that by the time I came to weigh out for the race in the afternoon, I needed a 3lb lead cloth.

Multigrey was owned and trained by a farmer called Godfrey Burr who lived near my parents at Sevenhampton. Richard used to ride for him when he could and was kind enough to stick me in for the ride on her after she had been declared to run in a Boys' Race.

Richard, or Pip as he is known, has been like a father to me throughout my career and was best man at my wedding when I married Miriam in 1976. Even though he has long since retired he is still one of my best friends and I am eternally grateful to him for the help he gave me during my early days. Apart from getting me my first ride and later on the job with Richard Head and Ken Cundell it was he who drilled into me the importance of making what money I earned work for me. The good earning years of a top jump jockey don't go on for ever, and when the day comes to hang your boots up it is nice to have something more than an over-worked liver to show for your efforts. It was also Pip who pointed out that riding ability was only part of what was needed to become a champion jockey, and that being tactful and showing trainers you are keen, are just as important. You won't get very far if you are riding for the King of Tonga and walk into the paddock and tell him what a wally he looks in a grass skirt!

As for being on the ball, ringing up for rides before anyone else was all part of the job, although I only ever once jocked another jockey off deliberately. That was following an incident at Chepstow when I was still claiming 7lb. I had just ridden a bad novice chaser and, after giving it a really good ride, got beaten half a length on the run-in due to the lack of my strength in the finish, which I was well aware of. When I came in one of the older claiming jockeys came up to me and told me point blank that he would have won on it. He was probably correct but I didn't see that it gave him the right to be hurtful. Myself, I would rather punch somebody on the nose than hurt their feelings and I made my mind up to teach him a lesson. I waited for almost 6 weeks before the opportunity finally arrived at Warwick. When I opened the *Sporting Life* in the morning I saw that the jockey concerned was engaged to ride an odds on shot in the Boys' Race but didn't have any other rides, whereas I didn't have a ride in the Boys' Race but did have one later in the afternoon. At breakfast time I gave Clive the money to telephone the yard where the jockey worked and leave a message to say that the horse he was due to ride that afternoon had gone lame and was a non-runner. I then made sure I got to the races early and made myself available to the trainer when it became clear that his jockey wasn't going to turn up. As I was the only conditional jockey there who didn't have a ride in the race, he had little choice but to use me. The horse duly bolted in and I felt that I had put the book straight. I was slightly embarrassed later when because I had got on so well with the horse the trainer decided to keep me on it and we went on to win three more races.

Except for the installation of two showers that never worked, the weighing room at Worcester is the same today as it was when I walked into it for that first time back in 1970. It is a long wooden building built just on the side of the River Severn which I think is where the water for the tea comes from! The atmosphere inside weighing rooms all over the country is tremendous and I think that being in there with all the lads having a laugh is the thing that I will miss most now that I have retired. It is like a jockeys' sancturay really and nobody except them and their valets are allowed inside and, as a result, it is the ideal place to moan about your trainer without the fear of being overheard.

If anybody ever decided to bug a weighing room ninety per cent of jockeys would immediately become jobless. It is also the place for the telling of dirty stories and the playing of practical jokes, one of which I got had by one day at Southwell. It was about twenty minutes before the first race and I was sitting underneath my peg reading a newspaper. Then Jonjo O'Neill came over to me and said that when Alan Brown came in it would be a good joke if I made some remark to him about his mother playing the piano. Apparently she was a concert pianist and he had been really embarrassed when his local paper had printed a picture of him sitting next to her while she was playing. I waited for a little while until Alan was in the middle of a bunch of lads chatting, and shouted over 'Hey, Alan, I hear your Mum plays the piano and has got herself a new partner. How about getting her down to play at the Jockeys' Dance next week?' Even when he is happy Alan looks as though he has just lost some money and, with a really sorrowful expression, he told me that his mother didn't have any hands. At first I wished that the weighing room floor would open and swallow me up but then my embarrassment turned to anger and I went for Jonjo. Just as I got to him, everyone in the room including Alan burst out laughing and I knew that I had been had. It turned out that there was nothing wrong with his mother at all and that I had just been the latest of a number of victims to the northern jockey's new source of entertainment. The sequel to this story is that Steve Smith-Eccles and I tried the same joke at Stratford the next day on Bob Champion but after Steve had told him his mother had no hands, the joke went a bit flat when Bob replied quite unconcernedly, 'Oh, hasn't she,' and went on to talk about something else.

Friends like Steve Smith-Eccles are few and far between and during the last seven years we have had enough laughs together to last each other a lifetime. 'You might be dead tomorrow,' was our excuse for doing just about anything and in his case anyone we knew we shouldn't. We did anything from pretending to shoot cyclists from the car window with the vet's humane killer to pinning girls' tights to the coat collars of stewards, while the other one kept them distracted. Provided it never hurt anyone's feelings, we were game for anything.

For a long time Steve suffered from what he liked to call an over-active reproduction gland, for which he treated himself with a never ending supply of girls. I don't think he ever cured it but he certainly went a long way to satisfying it. He never had any trouble pulling birds and if I had had a pound for everytime he told me that he could have been a film star, if he'd been six inches taller, I'd have retired years ago. It was a standing joke with him on the many occasions we shared a room together that just before we were about to go out for the evening, he'd look in the mirror while combing his hair and say, 'I bet you wish you were as good looking as me, Frank.'

When he was single he seemed to take out a different girl every night and the following afternoon with the assistance of some unsuspecting jockey, whom he would pin to the valet's table, he'd treat everyone to a reenactment of the previous night's activities, complete with sound effects. In 1974 after an afternoon spent at Sandown with paper and a pencil he calculated that if he got all the women he had been to bed with and laid them out head to toe, they would stretch once around the paddock and half-way across to the silver ring.

The great thing about him is that win, lose or draw, he'd always be ready to enjoy himself and he has promised me that if I ever succumb to the pressures of training and get miserable, he'll personally come and tear up my licence.

The valets are just as much part of the weighing room atmosphere as the jockeys themselves. Jo Ballinger was my valet to begin with but when he retired in 1974 I went to John and Tom Buckingham and their friend Andy, all three of whom are really great fun and have looked after me well ever since. It is not an easy life being a valet and they earn every penny they get. They are always the first people on the racecourse in the mornings and the last to leave at night and being faced with a mountain of muddy saddles and boots to clean on a dark, wet winter's night when everyone else is going home isn't a job I would put on my worst enemy.

The thrill of getting changed next to one of the leading jockeys on that first day at Worcester dimmed somewhat when he arrived and began to inspect himself for crabs which he feared some girl had given him the night before. It wasn't just a one off incident either and getting changed next to him until he retired in 1976, was like playing Russian roulette as the valets don't always wash the tights after each day's racing and I couldn't tell the difference between mine and his.

I don't really remember much about that first race itself other than the fact that Multigrey won quite easily and that whatever immediate thoughts I had that I was a jockey were short lived. Just after I had weighed in I met David Mould and asked him how he thought I had done. 'You looked bloody awful,' he said in his Cockney accent. As he was married to Marion Coakes who had had so much success with Stroller I knew David from our show jumping days. Apart from being one of the best jockeys that I ever saw ride, he was also the most stylish and so I spared him the embarrassment of telling him that it was him I watched most often and on whom I was trying to model myself!

If I imagined that riding winners was easy I didn't have to wait long to find out otherwise. On my second ride which was at Cheltenham, and my first for the Governor, I broke my wrist. The horse was a grey called King Street and he was having his first run in a three mile novice chase. The combination of a novice jockey on a novice chaser at Cheltenham is the ideal recipe for a disaster and we duly parted company after we had gone little more than a mile. He didn't actually hit the ground but he made a bad mistake and as I hadn't learnt to let the reins slip through my fingers when that happened, he pulled me straight over his head. As I fell I made the natural mistake of putting my hand out to save myself and as I hit the ground I felt the bone break. Putting your hand out to save yourself is all right if you fall over when walking but it is not to be recommended when you have just parted company with a horse doing about twenty-five miles per hour. After breaking my wrist once and my arm twice within the space of four seasons the penny finally dropped and from then on I was tucked up in a ball ready to fall almost before the horse knew when he was going to make a mistake.

After a visit to Cheltenham General Hospital to have my arm put in plaster I went home for a few weeks and waited for the bones to knit. For some reason I have never been a particularly good healer and as a consequence always seemed to take a couple of weeks longer than other jockeys to get back in the saddle following a break. Even in those days I was never keen to ride until I felt I was well enough and it was probably a good thing in the long run that I was born with a low pain threshold. I have seen plenty of jockeys over the years return to riding too quickly following an injury

43

only to aggravate it so that eventually they have more days off than if they had let the injury heal properly to begin with. Richard Rowe, Mark Dwyer and Neale Doughty are just three of many jockeys who frequently dislocated shoulders for this very reason. Dislocating a shoulder on Chumson in the Welsh National was the most painful injury I have suffered whilst riding. It took me six weeks and hours of isometric exercises before I felt fit enough to ride again and fortunately that was the only time it happened. The three jockeys I mentioned all started to ride within fourteen days and, of course, there is no way that the muscles have tightened up enough in that time to hold the joint together under the stress of riding. Once you have dislocated it a second time you begin to wear a groove in the end of the bones and it becomes progressively easier to dislocate. At the time getting back quickly so that you don't miss a winner seems the most important thing in the world but the older I got the more I began to appreciate the wisdom of Phil Bull, the boss of *Timeform*. He once said that racing is the greatest triviality, which when you look at the troubles of the world at large, it is. What does it really matter that one horse has beaten another in a race around a big field when there are millions of people starving to death. Once you retire from race riding you hopefully have a lot of your life to live and it is ludicrous to start that time off with a limp or degree of arthritis just because you wanted to ride a winner somewhere before you were ready. Dick Francis still has to tie his arm to his side before he goes to bed at night because if he doesn't and he gets his elbow above his head while he is asleep, his shoulder dislocates.

Once my wrist was healed I was eager to have another ride. Paul Kelleway and Victor Soane were both injured and we had a horse called Well Spent running at Towcester. As Pip had to go to Wincanton to ride our other runners Brian suggested that I ask the Governor if I could have the ride, and he agreed. It didn't win but it ran quite well and, more importantly, got me back on the racecourse. My second winner and the first of the 575 I rode in all for the Governor, came in February on a horse called Osceola belonging to the Governor's aunt, Mrs Beddington. This was also at Towcester and I remember thinking on the way home that this was it, and there would be no stopping me now. But I was wrong.

Having ridden a winner and broken my wrist with the first two rides and then ridden another winner, I was well aware of how one's luck could change. What I didn't realise though was how often. The next time I rode Osceola was at Hereford two weeks later and I came close to ruining my chances of becoming a jockey for ever.

The whole trouble was caused by the fact that I needed to take two pee pills to do the correct weight of 10st 2lb and the fact that I had no idea of the possible harmful side effects of using them. The problems began when I was walking the course beforehand. About three-quarters of the way round I suddenly felt a sharp pain in the left side of my chest which lasted for what seemed a minute but in fact was probably only a few seconds, during which time I could hardly move. At that point it didn't occur to me what had caused it and, after sitting down on the grass for a little while, I felt a bit better. I didn't have any further pains then until I was legged up in the paddock. Just as I went to raise my legs to put my feet in the irons I got a terrible cramp in my hips and again the pain in my chest. As soon as I put my legs down the cramp and chest pains stopped, the problem then was how to get my feet in the irons without the pain recurring. By moving slowly and pulling my legs up with my arms I eventually got myself ready to leave the paddock but, by the time I arrived at the start, I felt as though I was going to pass out. During the race almost any movement at all brought the cramp back and although I thought I had done well just to stay on, the Governor, who had watched the race at home on television, was none too impressed. In retrospect it would have been sensible to have told him exactly what had happened but I didn't want him to know that I was as heavy as I was and it was April before he gave me another ride.

Two months without a ride when you are desperate to prove to somebody that you are better than they think you are is a long time and as horses ran with boys up that I knew I could ride the pants off, I began to despair of ever getting on the racecourse again. With this despondency came a gradual rise in my weight so that by the time I decided to give up any thoughts of becoming a jockey, I was well over 11 stone. On 22 April I phoned my parents to tell them that I was going to hand my notice in and that I would be home the following weekend. There was none of this, 'Why don't you give it a bit longer,' business – they just said, 'If you're not happy, leave and do something else.' When I went down to tell the Governor I was going, there was only the secretary Mr Elliott in the house. The Governor and the rest of the family had gone out for the day and wouldn't be back until late that evening and so I had no alternative but to wait and tell him at breakfast the next day. I told Brian at evening stables. The following morning when I went into the tack room to see what I was riding first lot, my name was down to school a horse who was to put me back on the road to becoming a jockey and to whom I shall always be grateful. Osbaldeston was owned by a charming lady from Itchen Abbas in Hampshire called Lady Douglas-Pennant. He had fallen in his two previous attempts to jump fences because he was more than a little ignorant and pulled like a train. He was a small black horse and only distinguishable from his full brother Sonny Sommers because he did not have a wart near the top of his tail. If the Governor had been so minded they would have been an ideal pair for a betting coup and fortunes could have been made by switching them as they were both very good horses but preferred totally opposite types of going and distance. Whereas Sonny Sommers showed his best form over three miles in the mud, Osbaldeston only just managed to get two miles and needed top of the ground.

For some reason Osbaldeston behaved himself that morning. He jumped beautifully and for him settled quite well. He usually bolted with people half way to Wantage after he jumped the last schooling fence. When I trotted back to the Governor he told me that as he had jumped and settled so well I could ride him when he ran at Worcester the following week. I think that Brian had something to do with this, probably not because he wanted to see me become a jockey but because he didn't want me to leave. I had already given up doing my horses at evening stables and instead was employed doing all of the odd jobs in the yard from repairing the doors and broken windows to putting up an old staircase up to the hay loft. The Governor probably had similar views because he discovered that I was quite useful when his car wouldn't start and that when it did I was even more useful at collecting his daughters from school in Dorset.

We had two runners in the Boys' Race that day, the other more fancied one was an equally ignorant horse that Victor rode called Smooth Passage. Getting Osbaldeston to the start without letting him run away with me was my first and most difficult problem. On a lot of horses there is a knack of settling them but with him it was just brute strength, and keeping him at a sensible pace was like trying to pull a rapist off your mother. Once I had got him there I found the part of settling him during a race relatively easy and after keeping him at the back for the first mile I let him use his jumping to get himself into the race. We moved up to fourth place jumping the second last and cruised into the lead going into the final fence to win by an easy length and a half. The Governor was pleased and I was encouraged. In his prime Osbaldeston was one of the few horses who could match strides with Tingle Creek and until you got accustomed to the speed at which he jumped there was more than a slight chance he would cause you to need a clean pair of underpants for the next ride.

This win made me give up any ideas of packing in and it also did Osbaldeston's confidence the world of good. He won again for me at Hereford the next month bringing the total for my first season to four. The following season he was responsible for five of my eighteen winners and before he died in 1978, I had won seventeen races on him.

Once I had renewed my taste for success, I made my mind up to get my weight under control and go on a proper diet. Through Richard Pitman I made an appointment to see a dietician in London. He was eventually struck off the medical list but before he had his licence taken away he managed to make me and a number of other people feel very ill. He never bothered to ask if I had a weak heart or bad liver or anything. He just said 'You want to lose weight, do you?' I should have known then what he was like. A dietician has got to be pretty stupid to ask a question like that to a new patient. After he discussed the important points, like how much his fee was and how I was going to pay him, he made me take down my trousers and gave me an injection in the backside. He then went over to the other side of the room where he had three big boxes of different coloured pills and literally took a handful from each box and put them all into one big paper bag, telling me to take two of each every morning and to come back for another injection each week for six weeks. The tablets reduced my appetite and increased my metabolism to such an extent that after six weeks I looked as though I had just walked out of Belsen: I have seen more fat on a greasy chip. To begin with they made me feel terrific all day long until their effect began to wear off at about supper time when they left me feeling a bit flat. Then after a couple of weeks the ratio between the two began to change to such an extent that the high feeling was only lasting for a couple of hours and the remainder of the day I wandered about feeling depressed. To be fair to the doctor I did lose almost a stone but I felt completely washed out. In six weeks I changed from having bundles of energy to having so little strength that I needed to be in bed by 9.30 in the evening just so that I could do my job properly the next day. It took me more than five years to fully recover to the point that I honestly felt well again, which was when my finishes at the end of a race began to improve. It is a fact that although a lot of races are won by getting horses to jump well out in the country the majority of people only notice jockeys' strength from the last hurdle or fence to the winning post. And looking back now at some of the films of my earlier efforts in a finish it's a wonder anyone ever gave me a ride at all.

I have tried all sorts of diets and ideas to lose weight over the years but when it boils down to it the only sure way is to have the will power to stop eating. Sauna baths, physics and pee pills are just very short term methods of losing weight and as a rule once the effect of using either or all of them has worn off, your weight returns to what you weighed before you took them. Apart from making me feel weak I always considered sauna baths to be a waste of time and never took more than a dozen all the time I was riding. I resented sitting in a wooden box sweating my socks off when I could have been out in the fresh air getting on with something useful. I much preferred just to eat less.

The most unsuccessful diet I ever attempted involved taking a piece of fudge type food three times a day as a meal substitute. They were manufactured by a well-known slimming company and, providing you followed the instructions, there was a money back guarantee if you hadn't lost 5lb by the end of the course which lasted ten days. This seemed like a good idea as I stood in the chemist's in Lambourn reading the information on the side of the box and decided to take a course back to the hostel to try. I should have known what would happen when I read the line 'Tasty little cubes'. By tea time the next day I'd eaten the entire box and put on 2lb.

Bob Champion was, and still is, the worst person I know for kidding himself that he is dieting. He could walk into the canteen in the weighing room and scoff four or five sandwiches and then later on genuinely tell somebody and believe it himself that he hadn't eaten anything all day. He was also a bit silly. I was at his home one evening having a drink when a trainer 'phoned him to ride a horse with a light weight the next day. Anyone but Bob would have gone without supper and perhaps gone for a run in a sweat suit but not him. He went down to the chip shop in Hungerford for a large portion of fish and chips which he washed down with a Coco-Cola and then went home and took a physic.

The biggest problem with dieting is in the mind. To give you an example, if I ate a good lunch on a Sunday I wouldn't want to eat anything else for the rest of the day, but if after lunch a trainer 'phoned me to ride a horse with a light weight on the Monday, I would immediately feel hungry and want a sandwich or something at tea time. The week after I retired from riding I lost 4lb for no other reason than I only ate when I was hungry instead of eating when I could just because you never knew when you might next have to miss a meal. It is also quite interesting that in nearly all the falls where I sustained a bad injury I was at my lowest weight proving that going without food definitely slows up your reactions a little. The difference between being in a ball when you hit the ground and nearly in a ball is often the difference between a bad bruise and a break and one break can ruin a chance of being champion jockey.

Although after dieting I had my weight fairly well under control, there were still plenty of occasions when I would get to the races and have to resort to cheating in order to pull the correct weight. To be perfectly honest this is a silly thing to do because you are only kidding yourself and everyone else that you are lighter than you really are but when you have promised a trainer that you will do 10st 8lb and you get to the races and find that you are 10st 6lb stripped you have to do something.

I used many different ways of cheating depending on how heavy I was but the easiest one, when it was a very cold afternoon, was to take the sweat shirt off that I wore under my colours and then put it on again when I had weighed out. Under Jockey Club Rules it is permissible for a jockey to weigh in 1lb heavier or lighter than he weighed out. This is to allow for natural gains or losses such as sweating on a hot day or getting covered in mud on a wet one. But anything more or less than 1lb and you are liable to be sent before the stewards to explain the discrepancy.

Once I had started cheating and realised how much better it was than going without my breakfast, I was reluctant to stop. From being just 1lb heavy I gradually let my weight rise by nearly 4lb and taking a jumper off wasn't enough. Unlike flat racing where a saddle can weigh as little as 1lb, the lightest saddle that can safely be relied upon to stand up to the strains of jumping is at least 3lb. Add to that your boots, breeches and colours and you will find that the lowest you can possibly get them all down to is 5lb and that is without the comfort on a cold afternoon of anything underneath to keep you warm.

The next stage of cheating after removing the sweat shirt was to use passing boots which are exactly what they sound like. They are made out of very thin soft leather including the soles and weigh around 12oz less than a proper pair of boots. The only problem is that once you have passed the scales in them you have to go back into the changing rooms and put on your proper boots because the passing boots, with their paper thin soles, are painful to ride in. If you are very nice to the Clerk of the Scales he might just let you weigh in $1\frac{1}{2}$lb heavy without reporting you to the stewards but if he notices that you are wearing passing boots when you weigh out, you will be in hot water because they quite rightly don't like to think that you are putting one over on them. If I needed to use passing boots on a wet afternoon I used to rub mud on them so that the Clerk of the Scales wouldn't notice that I had changed into them and made sure that I went out in a crowd of jockeys so that he was too busy to take much notice. Once I had reached the point where using passing boots and removing sweat shirts still wasn't enough for me to do my lowest weight, I then had to come up with some new ideas.

To begin with I used to take the girth and surcingle off the saddle and send them outside with somebody else. I would then keep my fingers crossed that the Clerk of the Scales never asked to look under the number cloth to inspect my saddle because they were well aware of all the dodges. It almost became like a game to see just how much I could get away with and on a dozen or so occasions I got past the scales without even having a saddle. I used to manage this by putting an elastic band around my thigh with a breast plate underneath it – and praying! The normal procedure when you weigh out with a breast plate is that the valet ties it into the girth and surcingle in such a way that it can be clearly seen under the number cloth by the Clerk of the Scales because all extras such as breast plates and blinkers have to be declared to him. Once he saw the breast plate he naturally thought there was a girth and saddle under the number cloth holding it on instead of the elastic band and the stiff piece of cardboard I used to resemble the shape of the saddle.

The first time I passed without a saddle I nearly got caught because the other jockeys couldn't believe that I would do it. When I sat on the scales and looked around trying to look disinterested in whatever weight I happened to be, three of them were poking their heads around the doorway from the changing room to watch. The Clerk of the Scales noticed them. He knew that I was doing my lowest weight and immediately became suspicious and asked me to show him my boots. Fortunately I wasn't wearing my passing boots because without the saddle I was light enough, and I distracted him from any further inspection by saying that the jockeys were waiting to catch a glimpse of our assistant trainer whom I told him had a new punk style hair-do. When eventually our assistant came to collect my saddle, which one of the other jockeys had sneaked out to me, he looked just the same as he always did with his cavalry twill trousers and cloth cap. As I walked back towards the changing room the Clerk of the Scales called me over and said, 'I thought you told me he had a punk hair do.'

'He did, sir, but he's just told me that the Governor told him to change it back or he would have to sack him.'

'Good for him, I think they're dreadful,' he replied, and that was the end of it.

I was eventually cured of cheating when I was fined

heavily two days running after being caught for weighing in well over 4lb more than I had weighed out. Once I had cheated to weigh out the difficult part was getting back in again. Between dismounting from the horse and reaching the scales I suppose I had on average about a minute in which to get rid of whatever it was I hadn't weighed out with. Considering that after a race the area surrounding the weighing room is littered with officials, it wasn't always easy to pass a saddle or girth etc. to someone, even though I always had somebody waiting and it only actually took a moment to do.

I had been caught and warned a number of times about wearing cheating boots but never anything more serious than that until one day in November 1982 when the jockey I had asked to take my saddle from me failed to show up because he had been cornered by a steward for whom he had ridden earlier in the afternoon. Having made my way back to the Weighing Scales I looked everywhere for him and, by the time I reached the doorway, it was obvious that he wasn't going to show. I then looked everywhere for someone I knew whom I could trust to take the saddle but couldn't see anybody. It was impossible for me just to turn around and walk back into the crowd and in desperation I chose the last man I saw. As I stepped through the doorway I shoved my saddle into the hands of a complete stranger and said: 'Here, hold this a minute,' and kept on walking. I then sat on the scales and with a lot of smiling and flattery about his new suit, which looked as though it had been made for someone else, got back in at 2lb overweight without being reported. As soon as I walked into the changing rooms I sent the first jockey I saw who wasn't in colours back outside to collect my saddle but, before I had finished asking him, The Clerk of the Scales appeared in the doorway holding it and called me over to him. Of all the people I had passed that I could have given my saddle to I had managed to choose the friend of one of the Stipendiary Stewards who had gone racing with him for a day out. As this wasn't the first time that I had been caught cheating the Stewards fined me £50 and the very next day fined me another £100 for committing exactly the same offence. That was £150 too much for my liking and so I went on another diet but, try as I did, couldn't lose any more than 3lb. Whether I was just thickening out as I got older or whether I just wasn't as keen as I used to be I am not sure but I wasn't prepared to eat any less than I was and so I did the sensible thing and I put my riding weight up to 10st 10lb.

CHAPTER FIVE

Fired with success following my two quick wins on Osbaldeston I was disappointed when the season came to an end in May, which was unique. From that year on the short break from the end of one season and the start of the next couldn't come soon enough once the Grand National was over and, when it did, it seemed to pass all too quickly. Graham Thorner was Champion Jockey that season with seventy-four winners.

Until my car hire business took a turn for the worst I had planned on a fortnight in the Mediterranean sailing a dinghy but I had to scrap that idea and settle instead for a week under canvas in the South of France. A group of us all went together. There were Joe Tanner, Victor and myself in one car and John Merchant and Jimmy Nolan from Fulke Walwyn's yard in the other. We set off from Lambourn at 5am and drove to Dover to catch the 9 o'clock ferry across to Calais. If I said thank God I didn't take a sailing holiday once, I must have said it twenty times on that crossing over to the French coast and hearing the ship's captain announce over the tannoy system that we were experiencing the roughest passage in his fifteen years aboard the *Hampshire Rose* did nothing to make any of us feel better. Within half an hour of leaving the harbour it wasn't just the white cliffs of Dover we were saying goodbye to – it was also the fried breakfast that we had made the mistake of having in Winchester on the way there. Almost everyone on board, including most of the crew, was sick but Victor was probably the worst. Even after we docked at the other end he still felt ill and it was two days before he was well again.

Without being aware of it at the time the crossing was setting the scene for the following six days. Within four hours of getting down to Salou which was the camping site we had chosen to stay at, we were all badly sunburnt. It was just about lunch time when we arrived and because of the cool breeze coming in off the sea we didn't realise just how hot it was. As soon as we had pitched our tents on the small square of gravel that we had rented we put our shorts on and went across the road to the sea for a swim. While we were lying down in the sun afterwards we kept telling each other to be careful not to burn but none of us took any notice.

I don't know why it is but when a group of young people go on holiday together, they all want to be the first to go brown. About 4 o'clock someone suggested going for a drink. As soon as we got out of the direct sunlight we could see the damage we had done and after a couple of minutes spent sitting on a plastic basket-weave chair we could feel it. Joe and Jimmy would have made a lobster look anaemic and the rest of us weren't far behind. Despite using any number of after-sun creams we spent that night sleeping very tenderly on a thin ground sheet and the following four days anywhere where the sun couldn't reach us. Putting trousers and shirts next to our skin was out of the question. By the time the soreness had passed and we were ready to sun bathe again it was time to make our way back to Paris in readiness for another spell of being Moby Dick. But fortunately the sea on the return crossing was like a mill pond.

When Vic and I came back from holiday we decided that we had had enough of living like sardines in the hostel and were lucky enough to get digs in Upper Lambourn with Dolly and Tom Smailes. There were six of us living there altogether. Besides Dolly and Tom, and Victor and myself there were also Dolly's daughter and granddaughter, Janet and Fiona. The human residents were greatly outnumbered by Dolly's collection of pets. Indoors there was an old fluffy cat called Pru who spent most of the day choking on the hairs that she had licked from her coat. Her favourite resting place used to be in the kitchen on the bread board where she'd lie until Dolly left the room, and either Victor or I knocked her off. Then there were Kim and Cindy who were two black labradors and had obviously been impressed by the 'one man and his dog,' series. At the slightest chance they would be out at the garden gate and into the field next door where they practised rounding up David Nugent's sheep. While those two were alive he had the fittest flock of Scottish Blackfaces in Berkshire! The only other animal indoors was a Myna bird called Joey who lived in the conservatory. Joey had the worst disposition of any bird I have ever come across and delighted in biting anything that passed between the bars of his cage. Victor tried for a long time to get Fiona, Dolly's grand-daughter to feed it grape pips but even at four years of age she was too smart for that! She has now grown up into a really nice girl but as a child she was a menace and loved nothing more than to hold sweets out for the two dogs and then eat them herself. She also loved to tell tales on Victor and me when she saw us nicking Dolly's homemade cakes. The remainder of Dolly's pets were kept outside in the garden. Charlie and Peter were a couple of pet ducks. Then there were a dozen chickens and Blaze which was Fiona's New Forest pony. Despite the mess from the chickens and ducks wandering at will through the bungalow and the general chaos that was caused by the other animals, Victor and I spent three happy years there. There isn't a landlady in England with a kinder heart than Dolly and, when it came to cooking, she was second to none. As long as Pru hadn't got to them first and eaten most of the pastry, her apple pies were the best I have ever tasted and when eventually the time came for Vic and me to move on, we both missed her. Vic bought a house in the village and I moved to Sheep Drove.

Even when you have only one foot on the bottom rung of the ladder, as I did, there is always someone waiting to kick the other one away. There have always been too many jockeys chasing too few rides, and if the Jockey Club didn't issue another Jockey's Licence for five years there would still be too many jockeys.

In my second season I spent most of my evenings looking through the form book and most breakfast times on the 'phone begging trainers for rides. I kept a list of trainers who didn't have a claiming jockey and as soon as I saw that they had a horse entered in a Boys' Race I 'phoned them.

After riding four winners for the Governor up until November my first winner from a telephone call came on a horse called Old Paint in a selling chase at Warwick. He was trained by Ken Pipe at Bridgwater and owned by Jenny Hembrow who now rides quite a lot under rules herself. I won twice more on him that season and five of my eighteen winners came from outside stables. As I became more established as a jockey the ratio gradually changed and, by the time I had retired, I had ridden more outside winners than I had for Mr Winter. Most of my early winners away from Uplands came from Ken Cundell's yard over at Compton. Ken was a real pleasure to ride for and a gentleman with it. He was one of the few trainers who gave every apprentice who went to him a chance to get on and always took the time to help and talk to them. He also had the rare gift of being able to run a successful and happy yard with the respect of all the staff and yet never once having to resort to raising his voice. Most of his estate at Compton including the Gallops were paid for by some shrewd betting on Ken's part. The facilities there are as good as any in England and I looked forward to my weekly visits. I used to go over on Wednesday and maybe school up to ten horses in the pouring rain which wasn't so pleasant. But afterwards Richard Pitman and I would go back to the house for a change of clothes and a hot shower and then breakfast. Roden is one of those lovely old Georgian houses with an enormous kitchen and breakfast was conducted pretty much as I imagined it was when the house was first built. We had ham off the bone and wholemeal bread toasted on an enormous Aga.

When Ken retired in 1974 and his son Peter took over, a lot of the fun of going to Compton seemed to disappear. I rode for Peter for a few seasons and won some good races for him but gradually the class of horse began to drop and I started finding better rides elsewhere.

I only had one injury of any real consequence that season when a horse called Moss Royal slipped up with me at Market Rasen. As it fell I was thrown towards the inside of the track and hit the backs of my legs on a concrete post supporting the running rails. Some ten years later the much safer plastic rails were developed yet there are still plenty of the old wooden and concrete designs to be found which to me shows a complete lack of regard for a jockey's safety. There has got to be something morally wrong with a system that could find the money to save Aintree Racecourse but says that the replacement of old running rails will have to be gradual because of lack of finance.

Fortunately I had gone to Market Rasen with D. C. Stanhope who was then Assistant Trainer to the Governor. Neither of us had a car that was working at the time and so we borrowed David Nugent's blue Mini-van. In a decent car Market Rasen is a miserable three hour drive. In a Mini-van when you are hungry and thirsty because you are *dieting* and your passenger is the same it's a nightmare. As we drove through Leicester on our way we tormented ourselves by winding the windows down and letting in the smell from the numerous fish and chip shops and went through a menu of what we were going to eat on the way home. Resisting the food in the weighing room canteen at Market Rasen even when you are hungry is about as difficult as resisting a blood transfusion from an Aids carrier and I managed to do 9st 13lb which was the lowest weight I ever did. Apart from badly bruising the backs of my legs I took quite a lot of skin from my shoulders as I came into contact with the rough concrete. I was also quite shaken up. The course doctor wanted to send me to Lincoln Hospital to keep me under observation for the night but once I had some sweet tea inside me I felt better and as soon as DC had ridden we set off for home. With bruised legs and sore shoulders sitting down isn't one of the most comfortable positions especially in the seat of a Mini. On the journey back I kept thinking that Sir Alex Issigonis would have been much better employed designing a comfortable seat rather than a transverse engine layout. By the time we reached Leicester the thought of fish and chips made me feel sick and to DC's credit we didn't even stop so that he could have some. In Oxford I was just beginning to think that we would soon be home when we had a puncture in the front nearside tyre. It was then that we discovered that we didn't have a spare. Anyone but DC would probably have contacted the AA for help and spent the next three hours waiting but he has more sense of adventure than that. Once he had made absolutely certain that the spare wasn't hidden anywhere he jumped back in the driver's seat and set off on the remaining twenty-eight miles back to Lambourn, wrestling with the steering wheel as the van maintained its newly balanced direction towards the verge. I have forgotten now but for a while I knew exactly how many drains there were between the service station on the Oxford bypass and the centre of Lambourn because that night I kept a count as we dropped into each one. It was three weeks before I was fit enough to ride again and got back just in time to ride my first double at Kempton on Cardinal's Error for the Governor and Louis Boy for Ken Cundell.

To be getting rides and winners for two of the country's leading stables in only my second season was incredible. Then as Paul Kelleway neared retirement Pip began to take over at Uplands and my rise to the top continued on the back of him. The more successful he became the more other trainers required his services and when he couldn't ride for them, he recommended me as a substitute. The situation suited us both very well inasmuch as I was delighted to be getting rides for lots of new trainers and in return I was schooling a lot of horses at home that he was riding on the racecourse. He also knew that as a friend I wouldn't be chatting the trainers up behind his back in order to get more rides.

While I was gaining experience riding I was also learning about trainers and the devious way their minds worked. Thankfully they aren't all the same but the honest ones are in a minority. The motto on the trainer's Federation Badge reads *Homis treatis ai aimle mushted*, which translated means owners should be treated like mushrooms – 'Kept in the dark and fed plenty of shit'. To give you an example, if a horse goes lame at home they have this mental hang-up that they are to blame. Horses can break down anywhere no matter how carefully you train them so when they do why not simply say to the owner 'I'm sorry but your horse has got a leg and won't be able to run for a while'? Instead they will confine it to its box for a few weeks until the swelling has gone down. During this time they tell the owner anything except the truth about why the horse can't run. Caught a cold, stone bruised foot, bitten by a mad dog – you name it, they've said it. Then after all this pantomime is over they run the horse and it does itself twice as much harm as it should have done.

They say that you can't buy experience which is just as well because if I had I'd have missed out on a lot of the fun. I was learning and a lot of laughs came from the mistakes we made.

I remember the first time that Jimmy Nolan and I went to Wye Racecourse. It was before the M25 and M2 had been started and like Folkestone the easiest way of getting there was on the train from Charing Cross. After we passed through Ashford the guard came through the station shouting 'Next stop Wye'. A little while later the train began to slow down and we could see the racecourse out of the window. As we were both in the first, which was a Boys' Race and we were short of time, we put our coats on ready and got our saddles down from the rack above our seats. Then when the train came to a standstill we left the compartment and made our way along the corridor to the nearest door. Before we got half way the train started moving again and I shouted to Jimmy to hurry up. We sprinted the rest of the way to the door by which time the train was gathering speed. Jimmy got

61

there first and pulled down the window so that he could reach outside to open it. It didn't occur to us why there was no platform just a long drop to the ground below. Jimmy stood on the edge wondering whether to jump or not so I gave him some encouragement with my foot and jumped out after him. We both landed in a heap at the bottom of the embankment. As we picked ourselves and our belongings up Jimmy said, 'Look, the train has gone three hundred yards down the track and stopped. We could then see Wye Station. I don't know why the driver had stopped prematurely but he had. I would like to say that the story had a happy ending but it didn't. Jimmy twisted his ankle when he landed and couldn't ride for a week and my horse slipped up on the bend.

Wye was notorious for the number of horses that fell on its tight turns. The ground didn't even have to be slippery for this to happen and a lot of jockeys slept much better when the race course was finally closed down.

Aly Branford had a really bad fall there one day. Four horses fell on the bend and Aly was catapulted over the running rail into the middle of the course. Apart from breaking his collar bone when hitting the ground, he also banged his head and was badly concussed. When the St John Ambulance man reached him he was really worried. Aly was lying there in the grass with his body convulsing. As he put his hand on Aly's neck to feel for his pulse he got a shock and suddenly realised what was happening. As Aly had hit the ground he had fallen across the electric fence that had been put up in the middle of the course to keep the sheep in and every other second he was getting six volts of current through his body.

One funny incident that happened at Wye had begun four days earlier at Ayr, when Jeff King and Johnny Haine had gone up there to ride on the Friday and Saturday of the Scottish National Meeting. Both Thursday and Friday nights were spent in the bar of the Grenadier Hotel across the road from the racecourse where rumour has it they drank until they weren't sober enough to lift their glasses to their mouths. After the races on Saturday the drinking continued on the plane back to London where they decided to spend the weekend in readiness for the journey to Wye on the Monday. All of Sunday was spent in a Club in Jermyn Street and not surprisingly they both had more than a slight hangover when they went for a hair cut the next morning. Being a racing fan the barber couldn't stop asking them questions as to why horses he had backed had been beaten and what horses they thought would win that afternoon. When Jeff got into the chair and the barber put the apron round his neck he said 'Now Sir, how would you like it cut?'

Jeff looked into the mirror at the barber standing behind him and fixed him with one of his looks and said, 'in complete silence', and that was how it was cut!

The hangovers must have worn off shortly afterwards because apparently the drinking resumed on the train to the races. As they both only had one ride each in the second race they decided to catch the early train back to town but when Jeff returned to the weighing room and got changed ready to leave he couldn't find Johnny who, it turned out, had fallen at the last hurdle. When Jeff went across to the ambulance room he found John lying down on the bed looking as white as a ghost. Full of sympathy he told him to pull his finger out or they would miss the train. At this point the doctor came out of his room and told Jeff that John was very unwell and that he was quite concerned about him. He had been standing at the flight of hurdles where John had fallen and, as he hit the ground, had seen him being violently sick. 'Sick', said Jeff 'you wouldn't need to have a fall to be sick if you had drunk as much as he had in the last four days.'

'Drink' said the doctor, looking round at John. 'You didn't tell me you had been drinking.'

'You didn't ask me,' said John with his innocent boyish look, 'I kept telling you I was all right.' The doctor then had a complete sense of humour failure and threatened to report Johnny to the Stewards for wasting his time.

CHAPTER SIX

By the time I lost my claiming allowance in November 1972 I was riding regularly for a lot of smaller trainers as well as some of the bigger ones. When you have spent all of your time in the best yard in England where everything is done properly it does you good to go elsewhere and see how the other half lives. John Thorne who trains very successfully down in Bridgwater is a very good trainer but his facilities were a far cry from those I was used to at Lambourn. His seven furlong grass gallop is sited on the top of a cliff on the north side of his farm with a three hundred feet drop down onto the rocks below about fifteen yards to the left of the gallop. There isn't a rail! If a horse ran out with you while it was galloping I doubt if you'd even have time to jump off before it reached the edge and whenever I rode work there I always made certain that there was a horse between me and the edge. On one occasion I went there the fog was keeping the visibility to about ten feet and I refused to school.

Except for the protection of a thin blackthorn hedge which no horse worth its salt would think twice about galloping through, his schooling ground is just the same. When you've landed over the last obstacle you have approximately seventy-five yards in which to pull your horse up. If you can't you don't go over the edge of the cliff but instead drop 15 feet down Bridgwater's answer to the Derby Bank at Hickstead. Peter Scudamore and I watched Richard Hoare disappear over it one morning on a horse that was running away with him. We hadn't finished saying 'Christ, I hope he's all right when he reappeared going just as fast on the other side of the crevice. He then separated a flock of John's sheep before jumping the wire fence and galloped out

One of my most prized possessions – the Railfreight National Hunt Jump Jockey World Champion Trophy. This bronze was made by my great friend, former jockey and now well-known sculptor, Philip Blacker.

ABOVE: Victory in the Gold Cup, 1978.

BELOW: The Governor with Midnight Court's owner, Mrs Olive Jackson. *Gerry Cranham*

ABOVE: Me with my sisters Jill (left) and Norma – already too heavy to be a flat jockey!

RIGHT: The family, Mum and Dad with Jill (left), Norma, Sally the dog and me.

LEFT: Tranzy at the Marlborough Show on Easter Monday 1963 where we won five prizes. *Wiltshire Newspapers*

ABOVE: The VWH team which won the Prince Philip games at Castle Cary. I am second from the right on Willy Wagtail and my great friend Peter Wightman is second from the left on Silver.

Evening Post

LEFT: Red Paul and me negotiating the Hickstead Bank in the British Jumping Derby, 1970.

Findlay Davidson

RIGHT: Cleaning up on Willy Wagtail – winning the Anti-Litter Race at Swindon, Whit Monday 1965. *Wiltshire Newspapers*

ABOVE: Steve Smith-Eccles and me relaxing in Portugal.

BELOW: Riding against each other at Newbury with Steve on the far side.

ABOVE: Osbaldeston... the horse to whom I owe everything.

BELOW: Stratford 1973. I am on Sonny Sommers and in close pursuit of David Mould – by that time my style was beginning to improve.

Early days at Uplands. I am riding
Credibility and must be praying that his
blinkers don't slip over his eyes. *Gerry Cranham*

Grand National 1979 and a typical problem at the Chair. Andy Turnell (20) riding shorter than ever and Colin Tinkler trying for a place in the gymnastics team. I am in the background on Rough and Tumble.

ABOVE: Uncle Bing – one of the safest and best mannered horses I ever rode.

BELOW: Border Incident who, in his day, was the best 'chaser I rode. *Gerry Cranham*

ABOVE: This is what Captain Tim Forster would call a typical jumping day in March. I am (left) riding Carved Opal with Peter Hobbs on Brave Hussar. *Peter Hobbs*

BELOW: The red bungalow. *Miriam Francome*

At the Sportsman's Club with Telly Savalas after being Champion Jockey in 1976. *Alan F. Raymond*

LEFT: The Dealer who, without injury, could have been a really great 'chaser. *Sporting Pictures UK*

RIGHT: (Right) Lanzarote – another of the great horses I rode when I took over from Richard Pitman. *Gerry Cranham*

BELOW: Bula (nearest to the camera), one of the great Uplands horses. *Gerry Cranham*

Me and Peter Scudamore (right) in a novice chase at Kempton. I can't remember whether I am picking my whip up to hit it or 'calling a cab'. *Gerry Cranham*

LEFT: Sea Pigeon – the best hurdler I ever sat on and on which I won the Champion Hurdle in 1981. *Gerry Cranham*

RIGHT: The Governor. *Gerry Cranham*

Riding my thousandth winner – Worcester, 29 February 1984. Observe passes the post. *Pat Larkin*

All part of a day's work – being interviewed for radio.

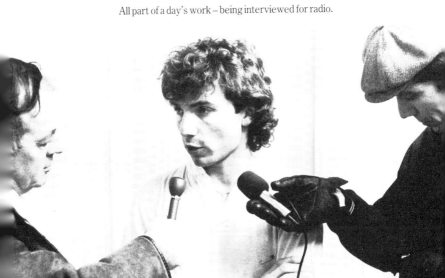

On 9 November 1984 I beat Josh Gifford's eighteen-year-old record of the fastest fifty winners.

Gerry Cranham

LEFT: Richard Pitman was best man at our wedding; in front of him is my mother.   *Gerry Cranham*

TOP: Miriam.   *Gerry Cranham*

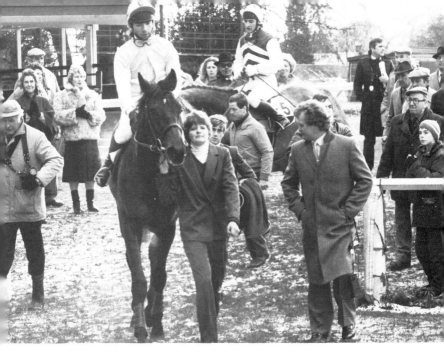

Wing and a Prayer – one of the many examples of John Jenkins' fine skills as a trainer.

Organising business at home over breakfast.

ABOVE: My 1036th winner, Don't Touch, which took me past Stan Mellor's record. *Gerry Cranham*

BELOW: The team at home. Left to right, Lesley, Joe (head lad), Toni, Angy, Miriam and Bruin the dog.

of view over the edge of we didn't know what. John told us not to worry about him because the horse did the same thing each time it schooled and Richard knew where he was going.

'What's his name?' I asked.

'What do you want to know for?' said John.

'Because when Peter and I see him entered to run somewhere we've decided to make sure we go to another meeting.'

The one thing I was always strict about when I schooled for different trainers was that the irons were big enough for my feet to slide in and out of. If they were too tight I insisted they were changed. I got hung up and dragged when I was a child and it frightened me to death. From then on I took every precaution to prevent it happening again. I don't even let anyone use my indoor school if they are wearing plimsolls or wellingtons.

When I got hung up on The Reject at Cheltenham in March 1985 it was one of only two occasions I have ever been terrified on a horse. It was just a freak accident. What actually happened was so difficult to reconstruct in the weighing room without the horse that the chances of it happening must have been over one million to one. As the horse hit the ground he rolled over to the right and I came off him with my left foot still in the iron. As we parted company I sensed a horse galloping behind me and tucked my knees up to my chest to make myself smaller. While this was happening we were both still sliding along the ground with The Reject going the faster and overtaking me. By the time the other horse had passed I could feel that my leg was caught in something and instinctively grabbed hold of the reins to prevent him from standing up and running off. Once I had hold of the reins and looked back at my leg I saw that my foot was still in the iron and the leather had somehow managed to wrap itself around my ankle so that the harder I pulled the tighter it became. I only managed to keep the horse down for a couple of seconds before he jumped to his feet which left me hanging upside down with the leather cutting into my skin. Geoff Capes wouldn't have been able to prise my finger off the reins at that point. I knew that if the horse galloped off it would kill me. Nothing would have broken the leather and as we only fell at the second fence the horse was still very fresh and would probably have galloped for miles with me dragging behind it. The thought of what would happen if he jumped a fence didn't bear thinking about. With me hanging up by one leg and trying to keep myself balanced on the reins the horse started to panic. He ran backwards a few strides and then tried to rear up. While he was doing this I was shouting to the people standing nearby to come and help me. To be fair they were only fence repairers with no idea of the danger I was in and with no experience of horses. After what seemed liked ages but in fact was only seconds one of them held the horse while two others lifted me up level with its withers. They had to turn me around 360° before I became unhitched. I walked far enough away from The Reject so that he wouldn't walk on me and fell to my knees in the grass. I didn't know whether to laugh or cry and settled for swearing out loud that I'd had enough of riding. This incident could have had a very different outcome with a horse less sensible than The Reject.

I was due to ride See You Then in the Champion Hurdle in the next race but when I got back to the weighing room I was still suffering from shock and Steve Smith-Eccles substituted for me. I can put my hand on my heart and say in all honesty that as I watched him sprint up the hill to win as he liked by ten lengths I didn't feel even the slightest pang of envy or jealousy. I was just thankful to be in one piece.

In my third season I managed to ride two more winners than my previous year and won my first good race on Free Thinker in the Free Handicap Hurdle at Chepstow. However the season came to a premature end on 6 March when a horse called Bentley Boy decided to jump into the ditch with me at Worcester. As he fell I put my left hand out to save myself and broke both bones in the lower part of my arm. It is a fact that you never have more pain than you can bear because when it gets too great your body cut out mechanism comes into play and you pass out. This said, as I lay there in the grass looking at the bone sticking out through my colours and felt the pain rushing in spasms up to my shoulder I began to have doubts whether my cut out system was working. When you are in pain the greatest sight in the world is a doctor walking towards you with a syringe full of pain killer. That wonderful feeling when your muscles finally relax following the injection is almost indescribable and if that is how drug takers feel when they are fixing or whatever it is they do, then I can really understand them.

Because both bones were badly broken the doctors in Worcester General, which is just across the road from the racecourse, decided to plate and pin them so that they would heal better and it was two months before I was fit enough to ride again by which time the season was nearly at an end. It seemed senseless to risk having a fall on my arm during the final two weeks and so I stopped and gave it the whole summer to heal completely. While I was off I had a leather support made for my wrist and arm which I wore until the day I retired.

I think it is the falls and the all too real possibility of being badly injured that creates the wonderful camaraderie amongst the jump jockeys.

I remember at Devon and Exeter one day when the Welsh jockey Granville 'Granny' Davis was making the running in the sixteen runner Novice Chase. His horse made a terrible mistake at the second fence on the far side and Granny looked like falling off. First of all he had both legs on one side, then momentarily got back astride the horse before nearly falling off on the other side. Eventually as he approached the next fence he got back into the saddle properly. If he had come off he would have had the stuffing kicked out of him by most of the fifteen runners because the fences there are very narrow but he somehow managed to get back into the saddle just before we approached the next fence. As he did so Granny's fellow countryman Johnny Williams shouted out 'Three Cheers for Granny, Hip Hip Hooray.' That sort of thing just doesn't happen in flat racing.

One of my colleagues in particular was always game for anything and up to every dodge you could name. At Chepstow once on a very foggy day he missed out all the fences up the straight and was laughing at the mistakes the horse I was on kept making. He then pulled back in to jump the last fence and rode his horse out to beat me for third place. I was so amazed at his cheek that I couldn't bring myself to object.

The 1973/74 season, which was my fourth, was the first that I managed to get a position in the Jockeys' Table. Admittedly it was only twenty-first but considering I broke my left arm again in exactly the same place, it was quite a good effort. The fall, which was from a horse called Maniwaki, was almost an exact repeat of what I'd done at Worcester seven months earlier except this time there were a few complications because I had twisted the plates. There is obviously no justice in this world because the fence before I fell I'd leaned over and pulled Geoff Shoemark back into the saddle after he had looked like falling off Zeus Girl. The accident happened at Wincanton which, if you have to hurt yourself, is the racecourse to do it. The doctor there doesn't make a meal of an injury by prodding and poking. He just looked at my arm as I was stretchered into the ambulance room and said "That's broken, I'd better give you a pain killer.' I was then taken to Bath Hospital to have the bones reset and new plates put in but for some reason the bones never really healed properly. Three weeks later I went to see one of the best orthopaedic surgeons in the country. Paul Aicroth had been recommended to me by Jean Cooper who along with John Scull and Ken Kennedy dealt with the many sessions of physiotherapy I needed over the years to get me back on the race course following injuries. Jean is a wonderful lady and has looked after me well throughout my career. However I don't know how she earns a living because she has never sent me a bill in fifteen years of visiting her.

Once I had been X-rayed and Paul had looked at the pictures he decided that apart from having the bones replated I would also need a bone graft from my hip to help heal them together. If I'd known at the time how painful the grafting operation was going to be, I'd have done without it. I drove home for a wash bag and returned the next day to London for my operation. I left the car in the car park around the corner from the Westminster Hospital and care of BUPA made my way up to the private rooms on the fourth floor. I'd asked for the bone graft to be taken from my left hip so that I would be able to use my right arm and leg to drive the automatic car home. As with all operations I'd had nothing to eat or drink for eight hours before and when I came round from the anaesthetic I was starving. I can't ever remember being so ill that I couldn't eat anything. As I lay there on my back with my left arm suspended from a hanger unable to move the only thing I could reach was an orange in a bowl by the side of the bed. It isn't easy to peel a tight skinned Jaffa one handed but I managed to scoff the lot in two mouthfuls. Five minutes later as I was being sick all over myself I wished I hadn't. Apart from the mess the physical action of vomiting aggravated my arm and hip and they both began throbbing. The following morning after breakfast I was feeling much better until two of the nurses came in and told me I was to get up and sit in a chair while they made the bed. As I put my left foot to the ground I got a terrific pain through my hip and I passed out. When I came round I was sitting in a chair in the corner. The pain had eased but I felt awful. Somehow the hip graft had gone septic and instead of two days it was almost a week before I was well enough to hobble back to the car. Teasy Weasy Raymond was in the room next to mine. He was recovering following an operation on his neck and I used to go in and sit with him in the afternoon and watch his TV. While I was there I also ate quite a lot of his fruit and chocolate.

The following season I finished tenth for him on Rag

Trade in the Grand National. The horse was trained then by Arthur Pitt at Epsom but, when he won the race the following season in 1976 with John Burke up, he had sent him to Fred Rimell. When I left hospital I couldn't put any trousers or shirt on because of my injuries. I made my way back to the car in just my slippers and dressing gown.

If I'd asked, my parents would willingly have come to collect me but I didn't want to drag them away from home on a Boxing Day and I thought I would surprise them. It was about four hundred yards from the hospital to the car park and by the time I had hobbled there I was looking forward to sitting down. Instead I was faced with a flat tyre. If it hadn't been Dad's car I'd have done a D. C. Stanhope and just got in and driven it home. As it was I struggled for half an hour with a jack designed by an idiot while the cold air whistled up my dressing gown. Eventually I changed the wheel and drove up the ramp to the pay kiosk where my luck changed. The old Indian man who took my ticket must have still been suffering from the previous night's festivities and instead of charging me for one week and two hours, he only charged me for two hours.

In fifteen seasons' riding I lost over four hundred and sixty days through injury which when you take into account the holiday periods is almost ten per cent of the total time. I didn't bother to count the overall number of falls I had, one was always one too many in my opinion and although I accepted them as part of the job I disliked them all. Now that I've retired, I certainly won't miss that horrible feeling when you are one stride away from a fence and you know that the horse you are on is going to gallop straight into it. When you're young you are saved this split second of agony because you haven't had enough experience to realise what is happening. The first thing you know is when you hear a terrific crashing of birch as half a ton of galloping horse flesh demolishes in a moment what it's taken a fence-builder the best part of a week to construct.

The crashing sound usually coincides with your mount's

head and neck disappearing from view as its back end suddenly finds itself travelling twice as fast as the front which forces it into a ball. If during the course of this action the horse can manage to extricate its front feet from the obstacle then the chances are that the front end will re-appear and you will be saved the agony of wondering whether he has chosen the same spot to land on as yourself. Having a big steeplechaser roll on you while you are on the ground is infinitely better than having it drop on you from about five feet. Once you've hit the ground all you can do is roll up into a small ball and pray! A field of horses galloping towards you while you are lying on the ground will turn even the strictest atheist religious even if it is only until the last horse has gone by. The three seconds or so it takes a field of horses to go past can seem an eternity and considering the number of aluminium shod feet which can pass over you it's a wonder there aren't a lot more serious accidents. Some of the more intelligent horses will try to avoid a jockey on the ground but a lot, like the jockeys riding them, wouldn't notice a family sitting down on a blanket having a picnic! To give you an example I had a fall at Huntingdon one day at the fence right in front of the stands. I landed about thirty feet from the fence and everyone, or at least I thought everyone, had missed me. As I went to get up an amateur jockey who must have been fifteen lengths behind the last horse with plenty of time to see me galloped all over my back and I couldn't ride for a week. The irony was that after seeing the course doctor I was cautioned by the stewards for using abusive language at the amateur as he galloped off towards the next fence. The other thing that happens quite often, which is just as annoying, is when you have had a fall and everything has missed you, you are lying there thinking how lucky you are as the sound of the runners disappears then suddenly the horse you have just fallen from gets up and tramples all over you.

Horses fall for all sorts of reasons but tiredness and ignorance are the two main causes. Intelligent horses with good jockeys rarely make a mistake, let alone fall but the combination of the two doesn't occur very often. For every natural jumper there are a dozen with hardly any co-ordination at all and the brainless jockeys outnumber the intelligent ones by about the same ratio. A lot of horses don't fall so much as the jockeys on top wrestle them to the ground.

The boredom which comes when you are confined to bed through injury is something else I never got used to and the following is an extract from my diary following a twisted knee at Chepstow.

'*Tuesday 24 April. 8am*. It's a lovely day and here I am stuck in bed with a bad leg waiting for my breakfast. Miriam has gone out riding and should be back shortly to get me something to eat. There are three hundred and fifty-eight red flowers on the wall paper in this room and a nasty looking crack appearing in the ceiling above the door. I've got three hairs growing from a mole on my stomach and I've also noticed a lot of white speckles on my finger nails.

9am. Miriam came back and brought me up a fried breakfast. There aren't any papers because they are on strike. Apparently a lot of moles have hairs growing out of them and the speckles on my finger nails could mean I have a calcium deficiency.

9.15am. Miriam has just shouted up to say that she is go-ing to see Candy Sasse and will be back in time to get lunch. There are fifteen different ingredients in HP sauce but no calcium. The aeroplane I made out of my napkin is now stuck in the curtains.

10.30am. Couldn't wait any longer. Having got up for a pee I decided to go downstairs and find something to do and decided to tidy the drawer where we keep all the odds and ends. Made a ladder using a packet of thirteen

72

amp fuses and some fuse wire and then found a good new game which kept me amused until lunch time. I got the box of paper clips and straightened one of them out. I then re-shaped it and put it back in the box and gave it a good shake. I then shut my eyes, tipped them all out on to the table and tried to feel for the one I bent.

When you are not well the best place to be is at home with your Mum and until I got married that's exactly where I went if I was ill and as you can see from my diary extracts I wished I could have done so afterwards!

Between the end of February, which is when I returned after my fall at Wincanton, and the end of the season I rode fifteen winners bring my tally for the year to thirty. Eleven of those thirty had been for outside yards including one for the late Fred Rimell and five for Captain Richard Head. I was very flattered when, during that summer, Mr Rimell approached me with an offer to become his first jockey. Before I gave him an answer I discussed the offer with the Governor who said that I must do what I wanted but to remember that Richard wouldn't be riding for ever. That was all I wanted to hear. I 'phoned Mr Rimell back to tell him that I was staying at Uplands and instead took a second retainer with Richard Head.

I first met the Captain when Pip Pitman asked me to go over and school some horses for him. He was supposed to have gone himself with Terry Biddlecombe but couldn't make it. As with the Governor I got started at the Captain's by winning on a horse that the senior jockey didn't want to ride. When you are top jockey and you've got sixty good horses to choose from it is senseless to risk getting injured any more than is necessary on a horse that, to all intents and purposes, has got a screw loose. The Captain's version of Osbaldeston was a small bay horse called Stone Thrower. He wouldn't have stood 15.1 hands even with new shoes on and was as thin as a herring. This wasn't anything to do with him being unhealthy, just a result of the fact that from the moment you got on him he was intent on running off with you and invariably did. As if being small, narrow and racy weren't enough he also had an extremely high head carriage which made the reins almost superfluous. I didn't even have to lean forward, to catch hold of the rings on the bit with my fingers. When it came to pulling hard this little lad was in a class of his own and after riding him Osbaldeston was almost enjoyable. I used to think he was going as fast as he could until a hurdle came into view when he used to change up a gear and go even faster. His saving grace was that provided you were brave enough to let him have his head he usually jumped well. Any effort to restrain him, however, brought his head up even higher than normal so that his nostrils were almost horizontal with his eyes. This impairment of his vision usually resulted in a long walk back to the weighing room.

The job with the Captain suited me perfectly. He had good horses, good owners and lived next door but one to the Governor at Rhonehurst where Oliver Sherwood now trains. This meant that I could go there to ride schooling at breakfast time without missing any of the work at Uplands as although I went to the Captain as first jockey I made certain that whenever the Governor wanted me I was available. I had a terrific time with the Captain and rode him over eighty winners in the first five seasons I was with him which, considering he had only room for twenty-six horses at any given time, was incredible. Of those eighty wins many were in good class races. I won the Topham Trophy and Mildmay on Uncle Bing, the Panama Cigar Final and Welsh Champion Chase on Border Incident and many others besides. Uncle Bing was a real gentleman and probably the safest jumper I ever rode while Border Incident, when he was right, was probably one of the best. Unfortunately he was plagued throughout his career with sore shins and never had the opportuntiy to win half the races of which he was capable. The one time he went to the Cheltenham Gold Cup one hundred per cent fit and ready to run for his life I managed to fall off him at the last open ditch when he was still running away.

King Flame was another favourite of mine. I rode my first winner at the Festival Meeting on him in 1975 when he won the three mile National Hunt Chase. He started at odds of 12–1 that day and would have been a lot shorter but for the fact that only I knew how well he had run on his previous outing. I didn't even tell the Captain what happened and the first he will know is when he reads this! I had already won three times on the horse that season and knew that he ran his best races when held up which is how I rode him at Doncaster in his warm-up race for Cheltenham. Unfortunately the whole course was shrouded in fog that day and having only ridden there once before I became disorientated while we were racing. When we approached what I thought was the third last fence I got something of a shock. As I looked across to my right I could just make out the shape of the grandstand and suddenly realised that the fence I was about to jump was in fact the last. Pegasus wouldn't have won from where I was so I just pushed him out with hands and heels and told the Captain that he had made a bad mistake on the far side and had been unable to get back into the race. It wasn't that I wanted to tell him a lie – I just didn't want him to know that I'd made a cock-up. It later eased my conscience that he wouldn't have won at Cheltenham with the penalty he would have got had he won at Doncaster.

I never really understood what went wrong at the Captain's but gradually the number of horses in his yard went down and, with it, the number of winners. It seems an odd thing to say but I think his success caused his downfall. The more winners he had the more nervous he became and the more he seemed to worry lest any of his horses might injure themselves. The only time during the season when he ever looked relaxed during working hours was when there was a foot of snow on the ground and racing was at a standstill.

When he finally packed up training and moved to

Salisbury in 1983 I was delighted for him. From a riding point of view I didn't want to see him retire as he was still providing me with winners but, as a friend, it was the right decision because it made him happy.

The 1974/75 season was really when everything started to happen. My riding never stopped improving right up until the day I retired but, by this time, I was beginning to gain some confidence. Until then I had been very self-conscious about my weakness in a finish and had made the mistake of admitting it openly. If I had had the brains to keep the worry to myself I would have coped with the problem at lot sooner than I did. As it was I got stronger as each season passed but forever had a doubt at the back of my mind if I had been beaten half a length as to whether I should really have won. Keeping myself fit to benefit my riding became almost an obsession with me. I was determined to be better than anyone else but I wanted to know it myself. There are only a small handful of people in racing whose opinion I value and if any one of them praised me, I was delighted. I was always my own worst critic. As for the rest, I never took any notice of what they said or wrote about me, whether it was good or bad. You can kid to others but you mustn't kid yourself is always something I remembered my father telling me. While I was riding I even had two operations on my nose and had my tonsils removed for no other reason than I thought it would help to improve my breathing while I was racing.

I remember the Governor telling me on the way home from the gallops when I was an apprentice that racing wasn't a game, it was a business. I think this piece of advice came after he'd seen me trying to pull Victor's foot out of the stirrup hole while we were riding work. Whatever the reason it was good advice and I always remembered it. Although I used to laugh and joke around with the lads and was basically happy-go-lucky, my work always came first. Looking through the form book, ringing up for rides and organising schooling mornings had priority over everything – just like thinking ahead from season to season, trying to work out which trainers could provide me with the most winners and organising my second retainer accordingly.

I finished the 1974/75 season with seventy winners, two behind Graham Thorner and twelve behind Tommy Stack who was Champion for the first time in 1972. Tommy was like me in one respect inasmuch as he wasn't really a jockey but a business man who rode horses. When he retired from riding and moved to Coolmore it was the equivalent of being promoted from the shop floor to the management level. Most jockeys when they retire just change factories.

Apart from finishing third to Tommy in the Jockeys' Championship and riding my first winner at the Festival Meeting, the 1974/75 season was marked by my first visit to the Jockey Club Headquarters at Portman Square. It followed a race at Plumpton where I had ridden a horse for Arthur Pitt called Boy Desmond. If the world had a backside then Plumpton Racecourse would be in the middle of it. At best the experience of riding there is unpleasant with its steep hill and tight turns but on a Bank Holiday Monday when you are one of eighteen runners in the Seller and the ground is as hard as the M1, it's terrifying. Over the last five years of my career I rode more winners there than anywhere else and I still loathed it. The Governor had more sense than me. He hated the fence at the top of the hill so much when he was riding that in the end he refused to ride there at all.

The Boy Desmond race was back in the days when the old wooden tote building in the middle of the course obscured the view of the hurdle on top of the hill from the grandstand. Otherwise there would never have been an enquiry. It has since been removed. I had been given instructions by Arthur to settle the horse at the back of the field and make my move from the top of the hill second time around. Everything was going according to plan when the horse just in front of me broke down and Chris Reed, who was riding it, pulled out sharply to his right to avoid jumping the next hurdle. His pulling out coincided with me making my move and, as a consequence, almost took me out with him. I'd been forced to pull back to almost a trot to avoid being carried out and by the time I got going again the rest of the field had almost reached the next hurdle and any chance that I might have had of winning had gone. Without using my stick and by just squeezing with my legs the horse kept galloping and did well to finish fourth even though he was beaten by more than twenty lengths. When I went back into the weighing room after explaining to Arthur and the owner what had happened one of the stipendiary stewards came in and told me that the chief steward wanted to interview me to see why I had left the horse so much ground to make up. I then repeated to him what I had told Arthur and suggested as they couldn't see for themselves what had happened behind the tote building, it would help if Chris Reed were brought up as a witness. The stipe agreed this would be a good idea and sent Arthur and me to the Stewards' Room while someone went off to find Chris who was getting ready to ride in the following race. Meanwhile the enquiry started and I explained what happened to the stewards knowing that when Chris arrived he would be able to confirm it. We then adjourned until after the next race, when Chris joined us.

Chris was asked by the stewards 'Do you think that you impeded anybody?'

'Not really, no,' replied Chris. I couldn't believe my ears. Chris obviously hadn't understood what the enquiry was about and thought that they were trying to put the blame on him for what had happened and defended himself by saying that although he pulled out he hadn't interfered with me. I then explained to Chris what the interview was all about, and that he wasn't under enquiry, but the damage was done and the stewards referred the matter to Portman Square. The following notice was printed in the next edition of the *Racing Calendar:*

'1975. Plumpton First October M. The Stewards of the Jockey Club enquired on November 17th into the report referred to them by the Stewards at Plumpton. Having heard the evidence and having seen the video tape recording of the race, the Stewards were satisfied that J. Francome had failed to comply with the requirements of Rule 151(ii). They also considered that the instructions which A. J. Pitt the trainer stated that he had given, were contrary to the requirements of Rule 151 and were contributory to Francome's riding.

The Stewards suspended Francome's licence for seven days from Tuesday, November 24th, inclusive and imposed a fine of £50 on Pitt.'

Rule 151(ii) states that the rider of every horse shall take all reasonable and permissible measures throughout the race to ensure that his horse is given a good opportunity to win or of obtaining the best possible placing.

When it comes to remembering offenders stewards make elephants appear like amnesiacs. Following the Plumpton Enquiry the words 'Francome, the stewards would like to see you' became all too frequent. There was a slight change, however, when in February 1983 the word Francome was prefixed by Mr. I have always thought that it is rude to call anyone by only their surname and one day when I was addressed this way at Kempton I decided I wasn't going to stand for it any longer. When the stipe came into the Weighing Room to find me, Tom Buckingham was in the process of pulling off my boots. The stipe walked over to where I was sitting and said 'Francome, the stewards would like to see you.' If I hadn't just been beaten on a horse that I thought was a certainty I would probably have just replied 'Yes, Sir' as usual. As it was I was already annoyed and said 'What did you say?'

'I said the stewards would like to see you.'

'Not that bit,' I said, 'what did you call me?'

He never answered my question but just ordered me to do as I was told. 'I'm not moving an inch until you either call me John or Mr Francome.' If he'd had a gun he looked as though he would have shot me but he could see that I had no intention of backing down and after a second of deliberating what to do, said 'Come along, John, we haven't got all day.' It nearly killed him to address me as John but he got the message. To his credit, he never held the incident against me and afterwards we actually became quite good friends. Had he brought this confrontation to the stewards' notice and any action been taken against me, I would have felt a real 'wally' because three weeks later and totally unrelated to my incident, the Jockey Club issued an authoritative stating that as from March 1983 all jockeys and trainers should be referred to as Mr. This was as a result of the bad publicity they received following a TV documentary about themselves which showed all too clearly the disparaging attitude of stewards towards most other sections of the racing fraternity.

Apart from my quiet style of riding I think the main reason I spent so much time in the Stewards' Room was that they quite rightly detected and resented the fact that I rarely took them seriously. This wasn't surprising considering some of the scenes and incidents I witnessed over the years.

The procedure at an Enquiry is that when you enter the room you stand before the three acting stewards who are seated behind a table. You are then formally introduced to each other by the stipendiary steward who stands to one side of the table and who is basically there to help the other three when they forget the jockeys' or horses' names or sometimes even their own! When they reveal the often mysterious reason why they have called you in, the jockey or jockeys concerned are asked to recount their opinion as to what happened. At this point it has been known for jockeys to suddenly become actors of Oscar winning standards and even your best friend can't be trusted not to lie through his teeth if he feels that by doing so will enable him to keep a race he is in danger of losing or alternatively pinch a race in which he has finished second.

Once each jockey has said his piece the room is darkened and a video recording of what really happened is shown with the horse concerned being indicated with the use of a

80

pointed stick. This in itself is often worth the inconvenience of an Enquiry as some of the stewards are so old they have difficulty in seeing the stick, let alone what is at the end of it. Before the lights come on again the jockeys are asked if they have seen enough or if they would like to see the film again. At Worcester one day after the stewards had insisted on watching the film through at least half a dozen times following a very reasonable objection I'd made to the winner, one of them turned and asked me if I had any further comments to make. I said 'Yes Sir, I've got two actually. The first is that I'm bored with this film and could you please put something different on and secondly, when will the usherette be bringing in the ice-creams and pop corn?' I recall that I didn't win that objection.

Once the video and comments are over the jockeys and a shorthand typist, who is present to record what is said, are sent out of the room while the stewards are left to make a decision, or at least that is what they are supposed to do. Personally from the experience I have had with them over the years I think that when the door is closed they reach a lot of their verdict by picking straws! If I thought I was seeing a lot of the stewards after the Boy Desmond race it was nothing to the comparative 'witch hunt' that followed the John Banks Enquiry. From then on I needed to do little more than blow my nose without using a handkerchief to be hauled before them. On one afternoon at Newton Abbot I had five rides and three of them resulted in my being called before the stewards because they weren't satisfied that I had made enough effort. When I walked into their room for the last Enquiry I asked quite jokingly if they would mind very much if at the next meeting I brought in my own chair as I was tired of standing up. My humour wasn't appreciated and I was ordered to behave myself.

While Steve Smith-Eccles and I were staying at the Palace Hotel for that Newton Abbot meeting we decided to go to Torquay and buy a couple of T-shirts to wear under our colours while we were racing. It was at the time when there was a big scare about the Herpes disease and we thought it would be quite amusing if we had something relevant printed on the front of them. Mine said 'You'll never be alone with a Herpes' and Steve's read 'Herpes rules O.K.' When Steve Jobar saw them for the first time he asked somebody if Herpes was a Greek God. I was wearing mine when I walked into the Stewards' Room at Plumpton the following week when Mick Masson and I were called in to explain the running of his horse which had started favourite. I thought that the stipe was joking when he said that the stewards wanted to see me as I had pushed the horse from start to finish in order to clear my lungs out. It was the first race on a Monday and I thought that the exercise would do me good. After I had explained to them that the horse obviously wanted either further or a much stiffer course we were shown the video which clearly showed that I had made more than every effort and that what I had said was correct. They were so far from the mark that it occurred to me they had made a mistake and had been watching the wrong horse and I felt sure that they would apologise for wasting my time. When it became obvious that no apology would be given and they were discussing the matter amongst themselves, I said 'Excuse me, but did any of you bother to watch the race or did you fancy just having an Enquiry and thought you may as well have me in as anybody.' With that Mick Masson was sent out of the room and I was given a severe dressing down and told that I would be fined if I ever said anything so impertinent again. I was tempted to ask them what impertinent meant but thought better of it.

Every day before racing begins the acting stewards are assembled and given a list of jockeys who should be watched during the afternoon but they aren't guaranteed to do even that properly. The following incident occurred one afternoon at Fontwell on what Captain Tim Forster would describe as a typical jumping day in March. The steady rain which started just before racing began got progressively heavier so that by the third race the ground had been turned into a bog. It was on days like those when the rain had got through everything except my skin that I cursed Judith Johnson for interfering with my education as I desperately wished for a job in a warm office. Instead I had just ridden a novice chaser having its first run over fences. After making two bad mistakes it turned a somersault with me at the fence half way down the hill and then the horse rolled me into the ground. Fortunately I wasn't injured but I looked as though I had just taken a mud bath. When I got back into the Weighing Room I was standing talking to John Buckingham telling him how the horse I had just ridden was exactly what he had been looking for to give to his mother-in-law as a hunter when suddenly a steward appeared and said that I was needed to explain why I had just pulled up because the horse I had ridden had started favourite.

'Pull up', I shouted at the state of my breeches and colours 'What do you think – that I got down and had a roll while I was leading it back?' The steward then went bright red as he suddenly realised that he had been watching the wrong horse and left.

One of the most enjoyable scenes I ever witnessed in the Stewards' Room occurred at Hereford when just for once it wasn't me who was doing the arguing. The person who was having a go at the stewards on this occasion was a permit holder from Wales called Bryn Thomas. An ex-front row forward for Cardiff Bryn was built like the proverbial brick lavatory with muscles in his spit and you needed to be either very drunk or very brave to upset him. Like a lot of permit holders, Bryn was a farmer who trained purely for his own pleasure and was the owner/trainer and box driver all rolled into one. I'd ridden a horse for him that had been well fancied in the very last race of the afternoon. For some inexplicable reason the horse ran a stinker and was never going well at any stage of the race finishing a well beaten sixth. It was early in December and by the time I got back to where the horses unsaddled, it was starting to get dark. After I had taken the saddle off I was standing talking to Bryn explaining that I thought the horse must have just had an off day when a stipe came over and said that the stewards would like to see us both. 'What about?' asked Bryn.

'They would just like to see if you can account for the reason your horse ran so badly,' replied the stipe.

'Listen, mate,' answer Bryn, 'just tell them I haven't got a clue and that I am in a hurry to get home.'

'I'm sorry, Mr Thomas, but they would like to see you.'

With that Bryn told him to hurry up and stomped off towards the Stewards' Room. It was another ten minutes before the stewards were ready to see us by which time Bryn was impatient to be on his way back to Wales and just beginning to boil up.

I've already explained the formal procedure when somebody enters the Stewards' Room so you can imagine for yourself the look of shock on the three faces of the men sitting behind the table when Bryn stormed in and slapped his cap down in front of them and demanded to know why they were wasting his time. Neither of them looked as though they wanted to argue with him and one told him tactfully that even the running of the Queen's horses were enquired into from time to time. 'Aye, I know,' said Bryn, 'but when she gets home afterwards she hasn't got to milk seventy fucking cows.' This was too much for me and I burst out laughing. Thankfully the stewards saw the funny side of it as well and calmed Bryn down by telling him that they would be as quick as possible.

Having recounted just a few of the many brushes I have had over the years with the stewards I am obliged to say that I wasn't always innocent. The business of failing to ride horses out in a finish for the minor placings was just a bad habit of mine born through laziness and a wish to save the horse from unnecessary strain. This practice resulted in seven separate appearances starting in 1975 at Towcester and culminating with an enquiry at Portman Square where I was fined the maximum of £2,500 for failing to ride out Easter Lee for second place. It may have been coincidence but this ridiculously high fine came only two weeks after I had referred to the stewards jokingly as 'the cabbage patch kids' during a speech I was making at the Race Writers Luncheon.

This isn't supposed to be a serious book so I won't go into the politics of stewarding and whether the amateurs we have at present should be replaced by professionals. I would just like to say, however, that as far as I can see the task of stewarding is a pretty thankless one inasmuch as if you make a good decision nobody praises you but make a mistake over something and everybody will be on to you like a ton of bricks.

CHAPTER SEVEN

My biggest pleasure when I took over from Pip was giving up my duties as a stable lad. Up until then I'd been mucking out two or three horses every morning and doing odd jobs at evening stables whenever I wasn't away racing. I didn't mind repairing the doors and doing odd jobs, but I've always hated mucking out and the awful smell that it leaves on your clothes afterwards. The only good thing is that when you have just mucked out three dirty horses on a wet morning you don't have any trouble getting to the front of the queue in the village supermarket at breakfast time.

As I was at last starting to earn some decent money I decided it would be a sensible idea to leave Dolly's and buy a house of my own. There are hundreds of 'favourite today, forgotten tomorrow jockeys' about and although I had no intention of becoming one of the latter you can't be certain of anything in racing.

Through a friend of mine called Sparky Thompson who does most of the dry cleaning in Lambourn I heard about a corrugated iron bungalow that was for sale within two miles of Uplands. If this was a fictional book somebody would probably write that it was exactly what I had always dreamed of and fell in love with it at first sight. But in real life people don't fall in love with corrugated iron bungalows especially if they are bright red! The only thing I did fall in love with however was its price of £8,000 which, considering it was set in one third of an acre on its own, seemed quite reasonable so with a loan from my parents I bought it. There wasn't any possibility of obtaining a mortgage because although it was sound enough it wasn't deemed to be built of solid construction. The inside was made of matchboard and when

I moved in on my own during the summer, there was quite a lot of work that needed to be done. The moron who designed the place back in 1920 must have had the hygienic standards of a skunk and the modesty of a cat. Apart from the Weighing Room at Sedgefield, the bungalow contained the only kitchen I had ever seen that boasted a lavatory and until I changed the layout it was possible for me to sit on it, answer the back door and butter my toast all at the same time! Something else that I had to replace were the night storage heaters that cost an arm and a leg to run. I remember my first electricity bill arriving and after looking straight at the amount at the bottom thought that somebody was putting in a bid for the place. A lot of the less important jobs, such as putting a lock on the back door and hanging curtains, which I intended to do after I was in, never got done until Miriam moved in when we returned from our honeymoon the following summer.

Apart from being Champion Jockey for the first time I will always remember the 1975/76 season for the most embarrassing error of my career. It took place at Huntingdon on 12 February when I was riding a horse for the Governor called Floating Pound. I had won the Embassy Chase Final on him three weeks earlier and although he started second favourite on this occasion to a horse called Summerville ridden by Andy Turnell, I still thought he would win. There were no excuses – I just made a cock up but to this day I don't know how I managed it. As we turned for home during the race the other runners were all struggling except for Andy and me and it was obvious that we had the race between us. I had only ridden over fences once before at Huntingdon and for some reason I had it in my mind that you jumped one fence in the straight and then pulled over to the left to avoid jumping the open ditch which is parallel with the finishing line. I now know only too well that it is in fact two fences that need to be jumped before you miss the ditch. As we landed over what I thought was the last fence I was about two lengths clear of Andy and going really well. I put my head down and rode for home aiming just to the left of the wing of the next fence so that if Andy was going to get to me he would have to come the long way round. About ten yards from the fence he drew alongside me on my right and for an instant I thought he was about to hit the wing head on. Then at the last moment he pulled over and jumped the fence. What an idiot, I thought, he has been forced to jump an extra fence because he was trying to be cheeky sneaking up on my inside and now he will be disqualified. With that Andy burst out laughing and I looked up. As I did so I could see the ditch in front of me and to my right and realised that it was me who was the idiot. In the instant I didn't know what to do and wished that the earth would open up and swallow me. As I passed the stands the crowd began booing and throwing things at me and I was in real danger of being lynched. When I got back to the unsaddling area I felt like leaving the horse and making straight for the car to avoid meeting the Governor and the hostile crowd that was beginning to gather but I needn't have worried. When the Governor reached me he just put his hand on my shoulder and said, 'Bad Luck, son' and that was it. I can't think of any other trainer who would have said that and I will always remember it. Suddenly the crowd didn't matter. At the subsequent Stewards' Enquiry I was fined £75 for failing to familiarise myself with the course which I thought was quite lenient. That evening I had the even more embarrassing task of phoning Mr and Mrs Boucher who owned the horse to explain what I had done and to apologise but they were just as sympathetic as the Governor. I couldn't afford to compensate them with the lost prize money but I did buy the Governor a china bird for his collection to the value of his missed percentage which helped to ease my conscience. The worst part of the whole incident was that the Governor finished that season with ninety-nine winners, just one short of the magical hundred which had so far always eluded him.

One other embarrassing incident that makes me cringe whenever I recall it happened at Warwick after I had just ridden a horse called He's Got It trained by the late Judy Miller. Judy was the 'Hattie Jacques' of National Hunt racing; just like the TV actress who was grossly overweight but had a lovely face and for most of the time was an extremely kind lady. However, when she became annoyed her voice level and vocabulary changed to something you would expect from a drill major in the Army and being on the receiving end of one of Judy's bollockings was definitely best avoided if possible. As a rule whenever I was booked to ride a horse I hadn't ridden before the first thing I did was to go through its form to try and get a picture of how it needed to be ridden and what distance and going it preferred. Having done that I would then look to see how it was bred and how old it was. For some reason the day I rode He's Got It I hadn't done any homework at all but had somehow got it firmly fixed in my mind that he was a young horse. During the race I rode him exactly how Judy had told me to but when I got to the second last where I was supposed to take up the running and go on to win, he ran out of petrol and finished a well beaten sixth. When I got back to the unsaddling area Judy and about six of her friends came over to hear why I thought the horse had run so badly. I explained that I thought he was a very nice horse but still slightly weak and just needed 'time' to develop. Judy bellowed at me, 'Time, you stupid boy. He's had more time than a watchmaker, he'll be nine next year.' Judy's comments must have been heard by half the racecourse and everybody within ear shot looked around to see who was getting the bollocking. I suddenly felt about two inches high and tried to come up with some feeble excuse but the damage was done. As I walked back to the Weighing Room trying to avoid the staring faces I vowed to myself I would never walk into a Paddock again without knowing everything I could about the horse I was due to ride. As for Judy she enjoyed every second of it and for a long time afterwards dined out on the story of how she had given the Champion Jockey the rocket of his life.

Ironically the season I took over at Uplands in 1975 and

became Champion Jockey for the first time coincided with the Governor's first defeat in the Trainers' Championship for five years. He was deposed by Fred Rimell who had won the Gold Cup with Royal Frolic and the Grand National with Rag Trade to bring his total winnings for the year to £112,000, almost £22,000 ahead of the Governor. The great days of Bula, Pendil, Lanzarote, Crisp, Killiney and many other Winter stars that had swept almost everything before them were over. Of the three that were still at Uplands when I took over Pendil was getting on in age and had leg problems while Bula and Lanzarote had really spent too long as hurdlers before being put over fences and, as a consequence, never jumped the larger obstacles as well as they should have. That said, I still won plenty of good races on both of them but because of their moderate jumping showed the sort of form over fences that had enabled them to win their Champion Hurdles. Sadly Lanzarote broke his leg when he fell in the 1977 Gold Cup fourteen months after I had gone to America to ride him in the Colonial Cup.

That had been my first trip abroad and although I didn't particularly enjoy myself the experience did me good. I travelled over with Mr and Mrs Winter and their daughter Jo. We stayed in Campden with Charlie and Betty Bird. Betty is a real star but I couldn't get along with Charlie. The four days we spent there were a continual round of parties all with the same people but in different houses and at some stage during each one he'd say to someone that he thought I must be queer or something because I didn't drink. Apart from this reference he virtually ignored me for the entire stay and I felt unwelcome. As for the race itself Lanzarote finished fourth to Grand Canyon but just the experience of riding in another country against different jockeys was good for me and when I returned to England I somehow felt that I had grown up a bit and had more confidence in myself. In 1983 I went back to Campden and won the Colonial Cup on a horse called Flatterer on whom I had won their big steeplechase the Temple Gwathmey three weeks earlier at

Belmont Park. Flatterer was trained by Jonathan Shepherd and owned in partnership by Bill Pape and George Harris. They are three of the nicest people I ever rode for and what Jonathan doesn't know about training isn't worth knowing.

I had been asked to go over originally because Jonathan had two runners in the Belmont Park race and John Cushman who was his stable jockey wanted to ride the other one. To say that you are riding abroad somewhere sounds really exciting but, like most other parts of a jockey's life, it's just routine and hard work. I flew out from Heathrow with TWA on the Saturday evening after having ridden at Ascot in the afternoon and touched down at Kennedy Airport at 9 o'clock local time. I had lost the piece of paper with the name of the hotel that Bill had booked me into and after trying to get in at three different hotels all of which were full, I ended up at a really shabby place about fifteen miles from the airport. It was so rough that I half expected to find gum shields for sale at reception but by this time I was so tired that I would have slept anywhere and took a room. When I went to the bar to get myself a drink to take to bed it was just like something from an American detective series. The room was dimly lit except for the lights around the bar itself and there wasn't a white person to be seen anywhere. Some of the women sitting up at the bar on stools were definitely on the game with imitation fur coats and mini skirts up to their arm pits surrounded by men wearing either woollen bobble hats or those over-sized cloth caps. I stood out like a sore thumb in my suit and if ET had walked in, he wouldn't have created any more attention. I got the distinct impression that I shouldn't be there and left as soon as I had paid for the drink. My room could only be described as squalid and if I hadn't been frightened of the possible consequences would have complained. The wallpaper was curling off the walls in the corner, the taps were rusted so that I needed both hands to turn each one on and there were pubic hairs stuck to the bar of soap that had been left stuck to the bottom of the bath courtesy of the previous occupant. I couldn't bring myself to look at the sheets on the bed – I just undressed, switched off the lights and got in. The next morning I 'phoned John Cushman to ask him to collect me and take me to the races. When I told him where I was staying he didn't believe me at first and was surprised that I hadn't been mugged because I had apparently ended up in one of the roughest areas in New York.

Belmont Park is quite a pretty racecourse with a small lake in the centre and lots of trees and has a grandstand that stretches half the length of the home straight. When I walked around the track before racing I was surprised how sticky the going was and decided that I would keep Flatterer to the outside where the ground was slightly better and where there was less chance of another horse galloping over me if I fell. John had told me in the car going to the races that one of the reasons he was riding the other horse was because Flatterer didn't always jump too well. As it turned out he never put a foot wrong but the better ground on the outside helped him. I was always going well throughout the race and caught the leader just after the last to win by a length. As I had a couple of hours to spare before catching the plane home I went to a bar across the road from the racecourse to have a drink with Jonathan and the owners and while I was there, agreed to go back the following month to ride him in the Colonial Cup. As time went on I 'phoned for a taxi to take me back to the Airport but it didn't arrive and so I 'phoned the hire firm to see what was happening. They promised that the taxi was on its way and ten minutes later an old blue Dodge the size of a bus pulled up outside the pub with a black man at the wheel and a woman sitting in the back. I don't know whether it happens much in America but this was the first time I had ever had a taxi call for me when it already had a fare. I told the driver that I needed to be at Kennedy Airport by 5.30 which gave him thirty minutes to get there and he assured me there would be no problem. It probably wouldn't have been if we had been in a helicopter and the woman sitting in the back with me hadn't lived on

92

the wrong side of a huge industrial estate. She quite rightly insisted on being dropped off first and an hour later, as my plane was taking off, we were all three of us still sitting in the taxi in a rush hour traffic jam that appeared to have no end. I eventually got to the airport at 7pm and refused to pay the driver. I had no idea when there was another flight back to Heathrow and told him that if I had to spend a night in a hotel, his company would be getting the bill. Fortunately there was another plane due out at 8.30 and I managed to get a seat on that. I arrived back at Heathrow just after 9am the following morning in time to drive to Leicester where I had five rides. To go to America for one ride on your day off is nothing short of madness and after I had won the Colonial Cup I only went back once to ride and that was on a four day trip to Fairhill as Captain of the British Jockeys' Team in 1984.

The trip to the Colonial Cup was even more tiring than the one I had experienced to New York. I spent the whole time on the move and arrived at Campden, which is a four hour flight south of New York, just two hours before my race. I got soaking wet walking the course and had nowhere to dry my clothes as the Weighing Room there is just a wooden hut with no light or heating. After I had won the race I didn't even have time to talk to the owners before dashing off to the airport, getting changed out of my wet racing clothes into my wet jacket and trousers in the car as I went. I was still quite damp when I got off the Eastern Airways plane and boarded the TWA flight back to Heathrow. Luckily the plane was virtually empty so I took all my clothes off and put them over the seats in front of me to dry off while I wrapped myself in a blanket and went to sleep. I never woke up until the stewardess shook me just before we were due to land in England which was quite embarrassing because at some stage of the journey I had lost the blanket!

I rode abroad quite a lot during the last five years I was riding and rode winners in seven different countries including the Italian Champion Hurdle on Shelahnu in Milan, but

France was my favourite country and if it hadn't been for the fact that I struggled to do all but their highest weight I would have gone there to ride permanently as Martin Blackshaw had done. The prize money there was high, the horses were good and the jockeys do virtually no travelling.

Switzerland was another pleasant country to ride in and an afternoon spent at Zurich Racecourse was as entertaining as any. They have eight races on the card made up of two trotting races, two hurdle races, two steeplechases and two flat races so that the crowd never gets bored. Whenever I went there there were never less than ten thousand spectators which would put most Group 1 English courses to shame. It was on the way back from Zurich that I had one of the oddest experiences of any of my trips abroad. It was my father's birthday coming up and as I was in Switzerland I thought it would be a sensible idea to buy him a watch. As it was a Sunday and all the shops were closed, I had to make do with selecting one from the Duty Free Counter at the Airport but nevertheless still managed to buy quite a nice one. Just as I was making my way back to check in a man of about fifty wearing a suit and carrying a briefcase came up to me. He seemed very friendly and said he had noticed me buying a watch. He then advised me that unless I wanted to pay the excess duty on it when I arrived at Heathrow I had better conceal it somewhere and suggested strapping it on my arm above the elbow. It hadn't crossed my mind that I would have to pay any extra on the watch and I had no money with which to do so. I thanked the man for his advice and went into the gents' toilet and did exactly as he had suggested. I don't know what the chances are of getting stopped going through customs but they are certainly a lot bigger when somebody points an accusing finger at you which is what this old bastard who had given me the friendly advice did. As I walked through the 'Nothing to Declare' exit he was standing with the customs officer and pointed towards me as I walked out. I couldn't believe what was happening and thought it was the dirtiest trick I had ever known. I could feel myself going red as a customs officer pulled me in and made me take off my jacket and roll up my shirt sleeve to reveal the hidden watch. I thought that if I ever saw that man again who had just shopped me, I'd wring his neck. The worst of it was the customs man wasn't content with me just paying the excess duty – he confiscated the watch altogether and said that I would be getting a letter to tell me when I could re-purchase it. I was still cursing my rotten luck as I stomped off towards the car park. Suddenly the little creep who had ratted on me appeared and told me not to get cross but to just stand still for a moment. He opened his briefcase and inside there were some fifty or so really expensive watches all much better than the one I had just had taken from me. He then told me to choose one quickly and so I took one which looked the most expensive and put it in my pocket. With that he closed the briefcase, said 'Thank you very much, you were very helpful' and walked away.

When I won my first Championship in 1976 with ninety-six winners I was pleased to have won but not ecstatic. I knew that I had ridden more winners than any other jockey that season but that didn't mean I was the best jockey riding and I was well aware that I wasn't. I was confident that I was as good as anyone when it came to choosing the right horse to ride in a race and I also knew there wasn't anyone better out in the country but there were still a dozen or more jock-eys who were stronger than I was in a finish from the last and it irritated me. I knew that until the day came when I was Champion and was also convinced myself there was nobody better riding I wouldn't be satisfied. I had to wait five long years and two further Championships before the day arrived but when it did it was well worth the wait. The 1980–81 season was the first of five consecutive years in which I rode over a hundred winners and when I dismounted from Rathconrath on 23 May at Warwick to give me my one hundred and fifth winner and my third Championship, I knew I had cracked it. During those five years I had been Champion again with ninety-five winners in 1979 and second once more to Tommy Stack in 1977. The other two years, 1978 and 1980, I finished second and fourth respectively to Jonjo O'Neill. When Jonjo broke Ron Barry's record of one hundred and thirty-two winners in the winter of 1977–78 it was the equivalent in achievement and effort to winning a Gold Medal at the Olympics and yet the day after he'd ridden his one hundred and forty-ninth winner to end the season as Champion and set the record, you had to scour the pages of every newspaper to find any mention of it. If it hadn't been for a catalogue of injuries keeping him sidelined Jonjo would have been Champion Jockey on a number of other occasions. I know a lot of people think that he ought to retire while he is in one piece but he's a tough little beggar and I personally can't see him packing in until he is Champion again which is where he ought to be.

Over the years I have heard it said about a number of jockeys 'He'll be Champion one day' but things seldom work out as planned and of those I have heard it said about, very few have managed to fulfil the prediction. Apart from the injuries which are inevitable there are a number of different reasons why jockeys who look destined to become champions don't make it. But the most common is because, like football, racing is a very fickle game. You only have to go a short spell without scoring a goal or riding a winner or just make a couple of mistakes and before you know what's happening, the trainer has started to look for a substitute. Which is sometimes ironic because a jockey's lean spell is often more of a reflection on the way his horses are trained rather than how they are ridden. It was this uncertainty that prompted me to make a decision at the end of the 1982/83 season.

I had started the season well and by Christmas had ridden twenty-five winners more than Peter Scudamore who was my nearest challenger. Then things began to go wrong. On Boxing Day I started to go down with some sort of virus which made it difficult for me to breathe when I was racing and which left me with hardly any energy at all. Just getting up in the morning was an effort and the only thing I looked forward to was the end of the day when I had finished riding and could go to bed. I should have had the sense to take a week's holiday but decided instead to try and work it off and, as a result, managed to make myself worse so that it was the middle of the summer before I felt really well again. From the New Year onwards the harder I tried the worse our horses seemed to run and almost everything I did seemed to be wrong. If I had the chance of two rides in a race I would pick the wrong one or if I had the choice of going to two meetings I would go to one and have a fall and miss winners at the other. Then, to cap it all, Sheikh Ali Abu Khamsin or 'Sooty' as I nicknamed him, decided that he didn't want me to ride his horses any more which came as quite a blow because he owned some of the best horses at Uplands. His decision soured me for a while because I had never done anything but good for the man and rode him a countless number of winners. The excuse he gave was that I had insulted him by choosing to ride Sea Image in the Arkle Chase for George and Olive Jackson instead of riding Fifty Dollars More for him. However, I believe the real reason was that he thought I had stopped Fifty Dollars More when I finished fourth at the Lambert and Butler final to Wayward Lad at Ascot the time before. The fact of the matter was that at Ascot his horse ran badly because he had sore shins and if it hadn't been such a valuable race I am certain the Governor wouldn't ever have run him. Racing a horse with sore shins is the equivalent of an athlete running with grit inside his plimsolls and it understandably drives them mad. He had always been a hard puller but that day was worse than normal and I dropped him in at the back of the field to make sure that he settled. He hardly took a leg off the ground at the downhill fences because he knew that landing was going to be painful and, by the time we turned out of Swindley Bottom, I had got some way behind. So I let him gallop home in his own time causing him as little discomfort as possible.

While I was struggling to keep hold of my lead in the

97

Championship Peter was enjoying a purple patch. David Nicholson, whose horses Peter was retained to ride, seemed to have winners every day and Peter was riding with plenty of confidence. When you are having a really good run like that everyone wants your services and, if anyone had a fancied horse running that they needed a jockey for, they rang Peter.

However much you tell yourself not to 'count your chickens' it is impossible to be twenty-five winners ahead of the second jockey and not imagine you have got the Championship won and during the ten weeks from Christmas as I watched my lead narrow to just three, I got as low as I had ever been. The frustration of working hard and getting virtually nowhere nearly drove me mad. Two of my few small moments of reward came by winning the Schweppes Hurdle at Newbury on Donegal Prince and then the Sun Alliance on Brown Chamberlain at Cheltenham which were both valuable races but at that time I would have gladly swopped them both for ten smaller winners.

A fall from a horse called Virgin Soldier at Newbury, which left me concussed on 5 March, was what finally tipped the scales well into Peter's favour and put him ahead of me and seemingly out of reach. It wasn't the compulsory seven days' rest that jockeys have to take following concussion that did the damage – it was the fact that the horse who brought me down had been ridden by Sam Morshead. Sam was first jockey to Mrs Rimmell and as my horse fell it rolled on top of him puncturing his lung and injuring him so badly that he was unable to ride for the remainder of the season. In Sam's absence Mrs Rimell made use of Peter whenever he was available and a stream of winners continued alongside David Nicholson's. With only five weeks of the season remaining Peter was twenty winners ahead of me and well on his way to being Champion when he broke his arm in a fall at Southwell. I remember sitting in the Weighing Room that day and being told by some of the older jockeys that I still had no chance of catching him, which seemed logical. At that time of year the jump meetings are few and far between and a jockey is normally lucky to get twenty rides, let alone twenty winners. I was still suffering from a virus and it was grabbing at straws but I made up my mind to have a go. I put in so much effort to try and retain my Championship that I felt I owed it to myself. On the way home from Southwell I began to think about Peter and how he must be feeling. I had been to see him in the ambulance room to make sure he was being looked after properly but now I was thinking what must be going through his mind. He had been denied a chance of winning the Championship the year before when a fractured skull three weeks from the end of the season had brought his run to an end. At the time he was only six winners behind and had every chance of beating me.

Now almost twelve months later fate had struck again. There are a lot of things that happen in life that don't seem fair and this was one of them. I decided that although I didn't deserve to lose my title he was certainly entitled to his share of it and that, if I did manage to drawl level with him, I would stop riding. Once Peter had his arm plated and was back home I phoned him to let him know so that he wouldn't spend the time to the end of the season worrying in case I should beat him.

It is when your back is to the wall and you are fighting that you find out who your friends are and during the five weeks that I struggled for my twenty winners I was disappointed by a few people but pleased by quite a lot. I spent every minute looking through the form book and on the telephone trying to get on horses that I thought had even the slightest chance of winning and ended up by riding winners for over twelve different trainers.

Ashford Ditton trained by Oliver Carter reduced the gap to nineteen at Ascot the day after Peter had his fall and then two days later I rode a double at Plumpton for Peter Cundell and Hugh O'Neill. Hugh's horse, Administrator, won the two mile Novice Chase but not before it had frightened me half to death. As we jumped off at the top of the hill it bolted with me and galloped straight through the first two fences which was for me one mistake too many. Going to the fence at the bottom of the hill I suddenly found that I wasn't so desperate to keep my title as I had imagined and decided that rather than fall, which was what I looked certain to do, I would pull out and miss the next fence. Apart from having no brakes I then found that I had no steering either. As I pulled on the left rein nothing happened and the horse galloped straight into the next fence causing it to land the other side on just one leg and it did well to keep its balance. Hitting the fence seemed to bring it to its senses and from then on it settled down and jumped well and won as it liked but when I came back I told Hugh and the owners that I would never ride it again, not even if I got to within one of Peter and it was odds-on in the last race of the season!

The next night at Taunton I rode three more winners, Solaroff for John Thorne, Cornish Granite for Martin Pipe and Sombrero for Stuart Pattemore. John and Stuart had been friends of mine for a long time and I knew I could count on them for help. When I got off Sombrero Stuart said that he would buy more horses if that's what it took for me to catch Peter and I knew that he meant it. As for Martin he is not only a very shrewd trainer but, like the rest of his family, he is a really nice man and helped me because he could see that I was struggling and needed help.

After Taunton I had to wait three days before my next winner which was for Mercy Rimell at Haydock on a horse that Peter should have been riding called Pirate Sun. I then drew a blank at Stratford and Newton Abbot before riding another winner for Martin at Uttoxeter on Lucky Eagle, followed by one more on each of the following days. One for David Gandolfo who can always be relied upon and who helped me as much as anyone and then one for the Governor at Warwick on a horse called Little Canford. This still left me with ten winners to find in only twenty days and the situation was becoming desperate. A double at Nottingham for David Gandolfo and Jack Hardy, another winner at Newton Abbot for Oliver Carter and one more on Easter Eel for the

100

Governor at Warwick took me to within six with two weeks left to go and for the first time I began to feel that I had a real chance. The following week I rode five winners. I made the long trip to Sedgefield for the first time to ride a winner for John Edwards on Buckmaster. I then drove across to ride a winner at Cartmel which is another course I had never ridden on before or since and rode a winner for Ginger McCain on Imperial Black. While I was there I also had a ride for Gordon Richards whose jockey, Neale Doughty, was one of the few who actually phoned me up to offer me any of his rides if I needed them. From the afternoon meeting at Cartmel I drove south to the evening fixture at Southwell where I won on another of David Gandolfo's horses called Upham Pleasure to put me on the nineteen and gave me a whole week to find just one winner. By this time I had driven over three thousand miles and could hardly wait to reach my target so that I could rest.

The following Monday, which was a Bank Holiday, I had four well fancied mounts at Fontwell and looked certain to reach my target. As it was I finished second twice, third once and then got badly shaken when Little Canford turned a somersault with me at the second last hurdle when he looked sure to win. With only four days' racing left I suddenly began to think that perhaps I wasn't going to make it after all. To get so close and not make it would have been cruel. The very next day – Tuesday 1 June – I was saved any further anxiety when I drove to Uttoxeter and won the Mayfield Novice Chase on Buckmaster.

The reception I got when I came in was tremendous and the Racecourse Executive kindly presented me with a bottle of champagne to mark the occasion. Once the celebrations were over and I had changed I went back to the car to wait for the other jockeys whom I had taken to the races. It felt more like five months than five weeks since that day when Peter broke his arm and the relief of having achieved my aim was wonderful.

I never understood the critics who thought that having

101

caught Peter I should have tried to pass him. (Perhaps they weren't lucky enough to have been brought up by parents like mine.) If they understood the ups and downs of a N.H. jockey's life they might never have questioned my decision.

One of the most enjoyable aspects of being a jockey is that you can meet a lot of nice people and, as it happened, I was lucky enough to ride for some of the best owners in England. A good owner in my book was somebody who, when they have met me in the paddock, looked pleased to see me and was more concerned that I and the horse came back safely rather than first. I would willingly give bad horses a ride for that sort of person and always tried my hardest but, if they were the other type who wanted to win at all costs and the point came in the race where I would have to risk my neck to win, invariably I didn't!

George and Olive Jackson, who owned a lot of good horses with the Governor, are really my type of people. When I walked into the paddock to ride for them George would slap me on the shoulder and say 'How are you, matey?' and he meant it. One of the Jacksons' horses, Sea Image, was amongst my all time favourites. He was quite a leggy horse and not the prettiest or the fastest I ever rode but, when it came to guts and effort, he was a dream to be on. As long as there was another horse in front of him he would never give up although his jumping sometimes hindered him. He was never really a natural jumper and on the stiffer courses like Ascot usually made a mistake that would cost him the race which resulted in his being quite well handicapped. So that when, on the odd occasion there was a prize worth winning on an easier track, he used to be something of a certainty.

Mr and Mrs Basil Samuel who owned Brown Chamberlin were two other great people to ride for and, like David Bott, Dr Brown and Vicky Phillips, could always be relied upon to phone up to see how I was if I was injured, which is when you really find out who your friends are.

The number of jockeys, owners and trainers who bother to do this were barely more than a handful and although I never resented the so-called friends who didn't, I would never go out of my way to help them afterwards.

The only people that I ever took a dislike to were those that talked down to me. It only happened three or four times and that was when I was still an apprentice but it is something I think that is unforgiveable and, although it happened a long time ago, I remember each occasion as if it were yesterday.

I may not have disliked many of the owners I rode for but I certainly managed to fall out with a few and in almost every case it was through betting. Betting, or rather losing money to the bookmakers, is the biggest undoing of most jockey/owner and jockey/trainer relationships which is just one of the reasons I had such an unusually long career with the Governor. Neither he nor the majority of the owners at Uplands ever betted and as a consequence when a fancied horse got beaten, it didn't have to be somebody's fault.

During my last two years of riding I had three owners accuse me of stopping their horses and, in each case, it was just sour grapes because they had lost their money. What really annoyed me about each one though was that none of the three concerned was man enough to tell me himself. They just gave some feeble excuse for not wanting me to ride for them again and I heard the truth from other sources. Then when the horses' later form proved that they were wrong, none of them had the good manners to apologise.

The worst of these were some owners who wrote to the Jockey Club without saying a word to the trainer or me to tell them they thought I had stopped their horse at Windsor and to ask them to investigate the matter. The first I knew was when an RSS man came to see me at the races one week later to tell me what they had done and to say that they were satisfied that the horse had been given every chance to win. They had seen video recordings of the race in question and the race before when I had won on the horse and had seen that I had ridden it exactly the same way on both occasions but that this time it just wasn't good enough.

103

Another owner told his trainer that I was never to ride for him again after he thought I had stopped a horse of his in a race at Kempton. He could tell you everything he knows about horses in under a minute but even he should have seen that the horse was exhausted when I got back in from the Kempton race. Without being hit the horse had given itself a hard race to finish fourth because it couldn't handle the very soft ground. When I told the owner this was the reason he had run so disappointingly he just grunted and walked away. From coming to my house and having tea we were now on nodding terms only and he avoided me whenever he could. He had told the trainer not to tell me that he thought I had stopped his horse but from the embarrassed expression he had whenever he was forced into conversation, I knew he wasn't certain that I didn't know. The next time his horse ran was again on soft ground. The trainer had two runners in the one race that day and, because of the owner's decision, I rode the other horse. It was pouring with rain when I walked into the paddock with the other jockey to join the owner and trainer under the owner's enormous umbrella. As we stood there huddling together cursing the weather I could see the owner fidgeting and getting nervous in case I asked him the obvious question of why I wasn't riding his horse. The trainer was just finishing giving the other jockey his instructions when the bell went for jockeys to mount and I decided I would put the owner out of his uncertainty. As the other jockey left the umbrella I called him back and said, 'You had better knock spots off that horse from the second last hurdle, otherwise you'll be accused of stopping him.' I then walked on and got on my horse. The outcome was that the owner's horse ran even worse than he had done when I had the ride and never ran a good race until he won on the flat on firm ground. Even then the owner never picked up the phone to apologise and say he had made a mistake.

The third and most disappointing of the three to accuse me was a man I have always looked on as a friend and we'd had some good times together. In his first season as an owner

I rode him several winners on some nice horses that he had bought in Ireland. I thought that one in particular was exceptional. He always worked like a very good horse at home but in his first few outings ran very badly. I then discovered that he liked to be held up in his races and, when ridden like this, bolted in three times on the trot. At that stage I really thought the horse would be good enough to take on the very best the following season and I was looking forward to riding him.

At this time everything in the garden for my friend was rosy. He had won plenty of money backing his horses and thought that I was the best jockey since Fred Archer. But then things changed. At the start of the next season the trainer decided against running the horse over hurdles and instead sent him novice chasing. He jumped the larger obstacles adequately at home without being brilliant and had his first run in October. Although he was short of work when he ran because of the hard ground we had had, I still thought he was good enough to win and, until he blew up going to the second last fence, that's exactly what he looked like doing. In the circumstances running short of oxygen was understandable but half way up the run in without me having been hard on him in any way, he began to whinny which is a sign of distress and often of a weak heart. When I reported what had happened neither the owner nor the trainer seemed particularly concerned and put it down to his lack of fitness but I had my doubts. The horse went home and seemed perfectly all right and was working well before his next run. However, he was dripping with sweat when I walked into the paddock to get on him and was unsettled at the start which was unusual. He then refused to line up and when I did eventually get him up to the tape, he whipped round and got left at least twenty lengths. I didn't rush him and just let him catch the others in his own time. Going to the second last fence I was 100–1 on to win when he suddenly went dead on me and began whinnying again. From going to win easily I then struggled to finish second and told the trainer there was definitely something the matter with him. I think that he believed me but my friend had a long face and didn't look too sure.

During the following three weeks before the horse ran again I heard separately from two good friends who had been with him when he told people that I had either lost my nerve or was riding for the bookmakers, and that I wouldn't ride for him again. The next time his horse ran, I decided to ride another horse in the race because I was convinced the horse was still ill. Most of the lads at the trainer's yard were also convinced that I had been stopping him and backed the horse as if he were having a walk over.

I don't know what would have happened if I had taken the ride for my friend but when his new jockey came into the paddock to ride him, his instructions were completely opposite to those I'd have given him. Instead of holding the horse up he made all of the running and rode him like a pacemaker. Turning for home he did exactly what he had done with me only instead of doing it at the second last fence he had done it four fences from home and he trailed in fourth. I did ride for my friend again afterwards and heard that he now knew I had been right. That said, I would have thought a lot more of him if he had told me himself. As for his horse I just hope that he recovers from whatever it is that has been the matter with him because he is a very good horse.

One summer another friend invited Steve Smith-Eccles and me over to Ireland with him to ride at Dundalk and we had two wonderful days. Des McGee and another friend, who, like Chris, had horses with the Governor, came along and so did Tom Norton and Noel Hiney. Tom manages horses for an Arab and Noel is a bank manager in London. Everyone of them seemed to drink constantly from the moment we arrived at the airport and yet amazingly never seemed to get drunk, just very merry. Noel's first words when we met at Heathrow before we had even been introduced were: 'Where's the bar?' Des had arranged for us

106

to have lunch with Bunny and Sally Cox just after we arrived and then we were going on to the races, which were in the evening. Des is an accountant and built like a bulldog with a neck the size of a normal man's chest. He was born in Dundalk and is very funny with a wonderfully dry sense of humour and had everyone in the hotel lift in fits of laughter. As we got in he put a really mean expression on his face and said as he pointed at his reflection in the mirror, 'So you're the bastard who has been spending all my money.'

The Irish are a lovely race of people with a wonderfully relaxed attitude and for most of them there is no rush to do something today if you can do it tomorrow. While we were having lunch at Bunny's I looked out of the window and noticed a horse that had got out of the stable and was wandering around in the garden. In England this would have been something of a crisis and would have caused people to start rushing around trying to catch it. Bunny just looked out at him and said, 'That's the fella you're riding this evening. Isn't he a good sort?' The horse was then left where it was until we had finished lunch which wasn't until 4 o'clock. About 5 I told Bunny that I had to leave because, having never been to Dundalk before, it would be sensible for me to walk the course. 'You don't want to bother doing that, John, have another drink and follow the other jockeys around. They'll know the way.' I did actually leave then and did as I planned but it shows the difference of approach between England and Ireland. An English trainer would have insisted that you walked all the way around the course and also that you didn't have a drink.

After the races where I rode a winner for Bunny but not on the horse that had been in the garden, we all went to the Castledown Hotel to a dance and to watch a beauty contest. We never got back to the hotel until four in the morning where Des, who had been appointed as tour manager arranged a meeting in the bar at 10am the following morning. The plan was to have a drink and then go sightseeing before the races in the afternoon, but at 1 o'clock after numerous more rounds of pleasure we were still in the bar. The sightseeing, which was postponed until after the races, turned out to be a visit to seven different pubs, not one of which was more than a mile from the hotel and Steve and I were only saved from visiting the inside of an eighth because Des had booked a table for dinner at the Hotel and we were all hungry instead of thirsty. During dinner Noel kept everyone in the restaurant entertained as well as ourselves by singing and telling jokes. I remember one of our party shocking one poor man who had never seen him before. He broke off in the middle of a song, went over to him and in a really appealing voice said, 'Lend me £50 until I see you again, pal, I think I'm going blind.' The following morning Steve and I had arranged to fly down to Tipperary to ride in a Charity Donkey Derby while the rest of the team flew back to England. We had been told that the plane would pick us up from Dundalk Airport at 10 o'clock and, as we were late getting up, decided to have breakfast there, but the airport turned out to be a field full of sheep in the middle of nowhere. The only sign of there having been any aviational activity at all was the dirty decaying windsock stuck to a pole and a rusty water hydrant that was useless because someone had stolen one of its wheels. At 10.30 we were still sitting in the field with no signs of life except for the sheep and were beginning to think we were the victims of a practical joke. Desmond O'Donnell, who was the man who had asked me to go to the Donkey Derby, was someone I had never even heard of before a telephone conversation the week before and the longer we sat there, the more the name sounded like something you'd invent. Suddenly we heard the buzzing noise of a light aircraft and saw it heading towards us. We then ran up and down a field scattering the sheep so as to leave a clear strip for it to land by which time the plane was circling over our heads. The pilot looked down at us and gave us a thumbs up sign in approval and then landed in a different field altogether. He turned out to be a part time builder who flew for fun at weekends and after watching him touch down on one wheel and bounce half way across the field, we both had reservations about getting in with him, but we did.

The flight down to Buttevant was fantastic and from the air you realised just why Ireland is known as the Emerald Isle. The donkey racing was a flop as far as I was concerned as my donkey was more interested in the ice cream a little girl was eating next to the ropes and refused to leave her when the starter dropped his flag. However, there were plenty of people there and Desmond succeeded in raising quite a lot of money for his charity.

CHAPTER EIGHT

If anyone can bring an out-of-form horse back to form it is the Governor. In 1985 and after a break of six years he regained his position at the top of the Trainers' League which, now that Michael Dickinson has retired, is where he deserves to be. I don't think that Michael was ever a better trainer of a horse than the Governor – he just put more thought into where he ran them and was better organised. In 1982/83 when Michael had twelve winners from twenty-one runners on Boxing Day and then trained the first five home in the Cheltenham Gold Cup, he caused most of the leading trainers in the south of England to worry even more than usual. They couldn't actually believe that there was a young man in Yorkshire who was making them look like complete novices and it was driving them insane, but instead of pulling their socks up which is what they needed to do, they just carried on as normal and did nothing but bitch about how lucky he was.

For someone who hates to be beaten as much as he does the Governor is the best loser in the world and was a real pleasure to ride for. He seldom complimented me when I had ridden a winner but on the other hand he never complained when I had been beaten on a horse I perhaps should have won on, and was the one trainer I rode for who never forgot from his riding days that things can go wrong in a race no matter how careful the jockey is.

In fifteen years I had rides from all the top trainers including Michael and I know that the Governor was the only one I could have stayed with as long as I did. He is basically a perfectionist and, where the horses' and lads' welfare is concerned, no expense is ever spared. The hostel may be cramped but the lads are always happy because they are all well looked after and know that the Governor cares about them. A lot of trainers don't appreciate that miserable lads will make miserable horses and when a horse is unhappy it won't ever do its best.

The atmosphere at Uplands is tremendous. Everyone who works there enjoys themselves but they all know that if they don't do the job properly they will get a bollocking from either Brian or the Governor. Whichever one of the two gives it makes no difference because they are as forbidding as each other when roused and, once you have had one, you try your hardest not to get another.

The pressures and worries of training good horses seem to affect most trainers the same way inasmuch as until the horses are safely back in from exercise they are extremely grumpy: the Governor is no exception. The nice man people see at the races and which is the real Fred Winter bears no resemblance at all to the person who trains the horses in the mornings.

Until 9.30 he can be as grumpy and cantankerous as anyone I have ever come across. Whatever anyone suggests he does the opposite and if the slightest thing goes wrong, he will blow a fuse and start shouting in a fit of temper. In the old days before hard hats were compulsory he'd take off his cloth cap and hit the side of his leg with it while he was abusing whoever had done something wrong. Nowadays he has to make do with hitting his boot with his whip. When he comes into the yard first thing in the morning and is in particularly bad form the message quickly spreads to the lads and everyone is even more careful not to make a mistake. I remember one such day in 1974 when the cause of his bad humour was the foul weather. The winter had really set in and there hadn't been any racing for over a week and, as each day passed, he seemed to get worse. The snow in Lambourn was preventing us from using the gallops and we were restricted to exercising the horses up a lane alongside Captain Head's yard in Upper Lambourn. Because it was

111

only narrow we used to trot to the top and then turn round as we were so that the last horse on the way up was the first coming back. On this particular morning I was about fifth from the front as we made our way to the top and the Governor was at the back. One lad had already been torn off a strip for walking over some ice and after we turned I decided to entertain the lads behind me by mimicking the Governor. I was doing the full works. I had my eyes shut to almost slits and my shoulders hunched as I made myself go red and mimed, 'You stupid bastard'. The more they laughed the more I continued and I then began hitting my leg with my cap to make my impersonation even more realistic. Suddenly they all stopped laughing and sat up straight. As I turned round in the saddle to see what had spoilt our fun I saw the Governor standing in the gap in the hedge looking straight at me. He never said a word but his eyes spoke for him. All the way home I waited for him to say something to me but he must have thought I was beyond worrying about.

I know that he won't mind my writing about pre-breakfast times at Uplands because he is the first to admit that he isn't at his best at that particular time of the day. I used to be terrified of him in the mornings but as time passed I got used to him and by the time I left I found his fits of temper quite amusing. One of the funniest mornings happened at the end of the 1983/84 season when the Governor and Neil Fearn and I were riding through Oliver Sherwood's yard on our way to the gallops. As we turned a bend in the driveway the Governor saw that the white gate to the rear entrance was closed and told Neil to trot on and open it. I watched as he dismounted from his horse and began inspecting the bolt on the gate but, by the time we had got to him, it was still closed. 'The gate's locked,' said Neil.

'Don't be stupid, son, of course it isn't, open the fucking thing.'

Neil then tried to bend the three-eight inch steel padlock that I could see was holding it. He grunted a couple of times just to let the Governor know that he was making an effort and then repeated: 'It's definitely locked, Governor.' With that the Governor took his glasses from his pocket and put them on so that he could take a better look. I can only imagine that the glasses weren't strong enough because after squinting in the direction of the lock and with a couple of more 'fucks' he insisted that Neil open it. Again Neil went through the motions of trying to open it but this time he was too nervous to stop. After a couple of seconds the Governor jumped off his horse and made Neil hold it while he dealt with the problem. If it was humanly possible for a man to break steel with his bare hands then he would have done so. He pulled and pushed and made all sorts of straining noises but in the end realised is was useless. He turned to Neil and shouted, 'You stupid bastard, it's locked.' I nearly fell off my horse laughing when he said this but he couldn't see the funny side of it. While the pair of them were getting back on their horses Alicia Head came out to see what all the shouting was about. She then explained that it was she who had locked the gate but that for some reason the key was with John Ciechanowski. She then suggested if we wanted to go through we could lift it from its hinges but not before the Governor had bollocked her as well. The whole incident didn't take more than three minutes and yet he accused her of ruining the entire morning's work. He obviously felt rather guilty about it afterwards when the real 'he' took over and I remember her telling me that he sent her some flowers to apologise.

The fact that I spent my entire sixteen years as a jockey with him is an indication of how well we got along and I can't pay him a bigger compliment than to say that I think of him as I do my own family. Like them, I may moan about him from time to time but if I ever hear anyone else doing the same I'll defend him to the hilt.

I think that the main reason we remained together for so long was because of the respect that we had for each other's capabilities. I never told him how to train his horses and he never told me how to ride them. He was always the boss and although he occasionally asked my advice as to where he should run a particular horse, it was always he who had the final say. We actually spoke very little. Once I had got off a horse after riding it in a race and told him what I thought, that was that. There was never any further discussions and never any continual moaning like a lot of other trainers when horses got beaten. My retainer to ride for him was always treated in much the same way. We never once discussed how much it was to be or even if we were going to be together again the following season. We just understood and trusted each other and at the end of each season I knew that however much was in my envelope would be fair.

We were basically as easy going as each other and never had one argument during all the time I was there. The Governor didn't even like talking about anything unpleasant that was happening at the time whether it be about stewards or phone tapping, or whatever. I remember coming home from the gallops with him once about two weeks after Rodman had been beaten in the Triumph Hurdle. There were only the two of us and just as we reached the track at the end of the gallops he said: 'John, somebody has told me that you were offered £5,000 to stop Rodman at Cheltenham.' Considering the conversation immediately before was about his car this came as a bit of a shock. I asked him who had told him, expecting him to say a man from Racecourse Security Services. When he said that it had been someone's dentist, I nearly fell off laughing it was so ridiculous. I told him that if he believed that he was going silly. He then went on to say that he didn't think it had been true but that he felt he ought to ask. True or not, if any other trainer had been told this about his jockey they would have had them in on the carpet and made a big scene about it not just casually mentioning it on the way back home from the gallops. Once I'd stopped laughing we continued talking about his car.

Rodman was only one of many horses I was rumoured to have stopped for the Governor and if I'd won on all of the horses that I was supposed to have stopped, I reckon I would have beaten Stan Mellor's record two years earlier than I did. In fifteen years at Uplands we never had one horse that did less than its best although I think Mrs Winter thought that I was stopping some of them from time to time. To be fair she never interfered with the running of the yard like a lot of trainers' wives do and we actually get on together quite well, but in my last year with the Governor I am certain it was she who was causing some of the friction that was creeping between us.

I was never fully convinced that he believed what I had said about Hazy Sunset who had run so disappointingly until it was proved to be true and then later on in the season he behaved completely out of character over a horse called Sailor's Dance. The cause of the problem was that Jimmy Duggan who had won on the horse first time out in a Boys' Race at Devon had kept the ride on him afterwards. Jimmy had only started at Uplands that season. I had recommended to the Governor that he should take him on because his parents owned two very good two-mile hurdlers called Aonoch and Amarach which were the type of horses of which we were short. I knew the Governor was keen to regain the Trainers' Championship which he hadn't won for over six years and thought they might help. As it turned out both horses left Uplands after only a short while but Jimmy remained. Jimmy is a really good jockey and if he had worked for his chances at Uplands like the other apprentices I wouldn't have begrudged him any of his rides for an instant. I was only too pleased to see the young lads getting on and all of the young claiming jockeys we had over the years benefited from spare rides that I put their way.

At Worcester, which is where Sailor's Dance ran after Devon, he was a certainty and I naturally expected to ride him. I had been with the Governor for sixteen years. I was Champion Jockey and had ridden three times more winners so far that season than any other jockey and yet I could sense that he was beginning to have doubts about me. When he stood me down in place of Jimmy, a 7lb claimer who had

115

been with him less than three months, I knew I was right. It wasn't missing the chance to ride a winner or losing money that upset me – I was just hurt and felt let down that he didn't want me to ride it. I have already said how loyal he had been to me but on the other hand I had been very loyal to him. I had never once asked to get off one of his horses in preference to ride something else with a better chance or because his was a bad jumper and never complained on the numerous occasions that he caused me to miss winners by changing his mind at the last minute about where he was going to have runners.

Sailor's Dance duly bolted in at Worcester and then won again on Boxing Day at Wincanton when I couldn't ride him because I had to go to Kempton. I then declined from having an argument with him when Jimmy rode the horse again in its warm up race at Ascot for the Cheltenham Festival Meeting. By Cheltenham, however, I had had enough. The Governor knew that it would be my last Festival Meeting and I thought that he would want me to ride every horse that had even half a chance of winning let alone a very good one as Sailor's Dance had. When he told me over the 'phone that Jimmy was going to ride the horse I wanted to know why and went straight down to his house to find out, but rather than have a confrontation and tell me the real reason, he gave in and said that if I wanted to ride the horse that much, then I could. I nearly told him where to stick his job there and then because that was just what I didn't want to hear. If I didn't warrant the ride on merit then I didn't want it. However, we had enjoyed too many good times for me to end our friendship in a blazing row which is what would have happened if I had insisted on getting to the bottom of the matter, and I only had a couple of months to go before I retired so I bit my lip and accepted his offer. When I went home and told Miriam what had happened she assured me I had done the right thing but at the time I had my doubts.

It was sod's law that Sailor's Dance would run a bad race with me at Cheltenham and then win again with Jimmy at

Liverpool the time after, but that's racing. I was never offered and I never asked to ride him at Liverpool; by then I had just resigned myself to the fact that he didn't actually want me to ride for him as much as he used to.

Now that I have retired the whole incident seems ridiculously trivial, and I'm delighted that we parted on the best of terms because I still have more respect for him than anyone I know.

CHAPTER NINE

Regardless of what the authorities would like to believe, the entire business of racing horses revolves around gambling and people's desire to have a bet. The thought of taking their local bookies to the cleaners is the ambition of every punter and it is their money that keeps racing going. The 'them and us' situation is just the same between a lot of trainers and bookmakers and in fifteen years of riding I saw more strokes being pulled in an effort to win money betting than Brian Johnston ever did while commentating on the Boat Race! Mind you, for every attempted coup that came off I should think there were at least half a dozen that failed which I suppose is why most of the bookies can afford to drive around in big cars while most of the trainers who like a bet cannot.

Regardless of what the average punter in the street thinks there are relatively few horses stopped through the course of a season and when they are it is rarely by a top jockey. Jockeys who are earning good money from riding plenty of winners don't need to take the risk of losing their licence through being stupid and, as a result, it is the middle-of-the-road jockey who is given the task. Then when the money is down and the horse is doing its best that's the time the trainer goes for someone better. It may sound odd but there are jockeys who win races and jockeys who just go round and go through the motions. The ones who are hungry for winners create their own chances to win in a race whereas the other type just wait for them to happen which is something I'll remember when I begin training.

I have never condoned the blatant stopping of horses by just pulling their back teeth out but I could never help admiring some of the other more subtle methods of landing a touch and often just the plain sharp thinking of some jockeys to get out of difficult situations. I remember a friend of mine riding a horse one day which had been the subject of a large each way bet. The animal had started at 33–1 and until it made a rick of the last hurdle the connections looked set to win a small fortune. From going to win it struggled to finish fourth and everyone thought they had done their money. However, between pulling up and getting back to the unsaddling enclosure, which took less than thirty seconds, my friend had persuaded the rider of the third horse for a reasonable fee not to weigh in so that he would be disqualified and my friend's horse promoted to third place.

One other jockey who was silly enough to be caught by a ring inspector whilst placing a bet at Newbury Racecourse was then extremely quick thinking. Just as he was placing the bet he noticed a steward walking towards him and ran away. This happened just before the 2 o'clock race. At the time the jockey was living less than three miles from the racecourse. As soon as he got clear of the steward he rushed to his car and raced home where he got changed into a completely different set of clothes. He then dashed back to the racecourse knowing that the stewards would be looking for him and sat in the weighing room as if nothing had happened. When he was called for and stood in front of the ring inspector he denied all knowledge of having been near the bookmakers and insisted that he hadn't left the weighing room since he had arrived. Seeing him in different clothes the steward who had spotted him began to have doubts as to whether it was actually him he had seen and was forced to give him the benefit of the doubt and let him go. Had he been found guilty he would have lost his licence for a long time.

Whereas it is relatively simple to plan a coup it's another story altogether to actually pull one off and although almost all who are involved in racing likes to kid themselves that they know when their horse is going to win, the really good judges are few and far between. 'It would have won but . . .'

is probably the most over-used phrase I know amongst betting people who will do anything but admit to the fact they have lost their money due to their own miscalculations. It's difficult for me to speak for the North of England because I seldom rode there but of the fifty or so jockeys who rode regularly in the South there were less than a handful who knew the time of day when it came to calculating the chance of a particular horse. Similarly they were the only jockeys who could be relied upon to tell you exactly how a horse needed to be ridden and what distance it wanted if you happened to ride something they had ridden before.

There isn't such a thing in racing as a certainty even if you cheat. A perfect example happened at Worcester back in 1979, although the story began at Ludlow about two months earlier when I noticed something very odd as I was walking around at the start of the two mile Handicap Hurdle. As one of the jockeys was having his girth checked I could see that he was riding on a very small saddle with a heavy cloth which is something that jockeys just don't do. To ride like this would be very uncomfortable and instead jockeys just use bigger and heavier saddles.

Had the jockey not been riding for a trainer who I knew loved to have a bet I probably wouldn't have given it much more thought but he was and so I asked him what weight the horse had. When he replied 10st 4lbs I knew that they were up to something because that was about his lowest weight and there was no way that he would need any sort of lead cloth, let alone a heavy one. I guessed what they were up to and watched as the jockey gave the horse every chance to win the race but with its extra weight it wasn't good enough and eventually finished fifth, beaten no more than six lengths by the winner. When it came to unsaddling the jockey conveniently left the lead cloth behind with the trainer and, when he stepped on the scales, pulled just the correct weight. I couldn't tell exactly but I estimated that the horse had carried about 20lb more than it should have done and presumed that the only reason they hadn't let it win, which it would have done with its correct weight, was because they were waiting for a bigger prize. From then on I kept a careful eye on the *Sporting Life* to see where the horse was entered and made certain that every time it ran I was there to watch. The next time the horse ran I was riding in the same race. I had taken the jockey to one side and told him that I knew what was going on and that I wanted to know when the horse was going to run with it correct weight but he insisted that until he actually got into the paddock he never knew himself. Apparently the horse had already had two runs with its extra weight before I had noticed it and the trainer wasn't going to take the chance of his jockey stealing the best prize when the day came for it to win. After two fruitless journeys to Hereford and Wolverhampton, where again the horse ran well considering its extra weight, the day finally arrived. The trainer had chosen quite a good selling hurdle race to land his touch and although his horse was set to carry 10st 13lbs it would have had over 12st 7lbs if the handicapper had known its true form.

Everything worked out according to plan until the very last moment. The horse had started at 10–1 and all the way through the race it was running away. Then going to the final flight of hurdles it looked to be home and dry but then it stood off the jump much too soon and fell. Luckily the only thing that was hurt was the trainer's pocket and although the horse won the next time it ran it didn't do anyone much good because its true form had been shown up and it started at skinny odds again.

Until 1984 'phone tapping was something I had only seen on TV detective series and read about in newspapers concerning matters of national security. Then suddenly on 3 March I found out it had been happening to me.

I had been riding at Newbury and until it happened I was in tremendous form. I had ridden two winners the previous day and had then won the opener on Park Rainbow who was my hundredth winner of the season. In the second last race, which was a novice hurdle, I rode a horse for the Governor

121

called Strike Lucky who was having his first run over hurdles. He ran quite well and finished eighth and, when I came back, his lad led me to where the also-rans were unsaddling. Just as I dismounted and before I had even turned around to tell the Governor and the owners how he had run, two really unpleasant-looking men aged about thirty-five barged their way between us and said that they were from the *Daily Mirror* and did I know my 'phone was being tapped? While they were saying this one of them shoved a tape recorder towards me and I could just make out the sound of my own voice. If they hadn't appeared quite so menacing I would have thought that someone was playing a practical joke, it seemed so ridiculous. Tapped 'phone or not I told them to clear off and pushed them away while I spoke to the owners who looked every bit as shocked as I felt. Once I had spoken to them the two men continued to pester me all the way back to the weighing room demanding that I made a comment. I said nothing but told them that once I had weighed in I would come out to see them. Strike Lucky had been my last ride of the day and so fortunately I was able to give the matter my full attention. Between weighing in and coming back out again I racked my brain trying to recall all of my recent conversations. I defy anybody to say that they have never said anything over the 'phone that they wouldn't mind being printed in a newspaper and I desperately tried to remember anything I had said that I shouldn't.

When I saw the two men later they were slightly less aggressive and apologised for being so rude. It turned out that someone, not from the *Daily Mirror*, had been tapping my 'phone since early November and had recorded over twenty-seven hours of conversation. The people who had done the tapping obviously hoped to hear me say something which would have made a tremendous scoop for the newspapers but in over four months the most sinister recording they had was one between myself and Stuart Pattemore. Stuart had 'phoned me because he had a horse running at Cheltenham called Return to Power who was a very strong puller. It was only ninety-five per cent fit and having its first run of the season so Stuart naturally didn't want just anyone riding it because he knew that if it ran away it might injure itself. As I was going to Lingfield and couldn't ride for him I looked in the paper to see who didn't have a ride in the race and suggested he asked Neale Doughty who I knew would be suitable for the job. I then told Stuart that if Neil agreed to ride he should give him £100 on top of his riding fee for his trouble because the horse was a horrible ride and not the sort that a top jockey would sit on from choice. From this the newspaper reporters who wouldn't know one end of a horse from the other deduced that the horse was being stopped which was ridiculous. It was 33–1 at the off which was a true reflection of its chance in the race and it wouldn't have been good enough to win if it had started the day before. When I finished listening to this conversation I asked them if that was the worst they had and they said 'Yes'. I then burst out laughing and told them to come back again when they had something worth bothering me with. At the same time that they had been talking to me they had sent three other teams of men to different parts of the country and one team to America to interview some of the people whom I had been speaking to. The way they behaved was extremely under-hand to say the least. They had arranged a meeting with Stuart Pattemore by pretending that they were prospective owners but, when they arrived, and told him who they really were and what they wanted he threw them out. The reporters who visited Neale acted completely out of order as well and tried to trick him by playing him the tape and then saying that I had told them categorically that he had stopped the horse. Luckily Neil told them the truth and that if I had said he had stopped the horse, then I was lying.

The other three people who were interviewed were all good friends of mine whom I had spoken to over the 'phone and with whom I had the type of conversation that I normally had with the postman. We just chatted about the afternoon's racing and which horses we thought could run well and that was that. They made up their own minds which horses to lose their money on and I certainly wasn't punting to them.

Alan and Cynthia Argeband who are my friends responsible for getting me hooked on tennis and Marcus Christodoulou who has a restaurant in Paddington both refused to have anything to do with them but David Wickins, who was my other friend they contacted, appeared much more helpful. He was over in America on business at the time and when they telephoned him to let him know that they had been tapping our telephone conversations he told them that he had quite a lot more information that they would like to hear but that rather than talk about it over the 'phone it would be best if they flew somebody over to see him personally, and arranged a meeting for 10am the next morning. I should think that David and the reporter must have passed each other somewhere across the Atlantic because at 9.30 the following day David was keeping an appointment in London. When the *Daily Mirror* realised what he had done they were furious but there was nothing they could do. He had given them a taste of their own medicine and refused to make any comment.

Although I told the two men at Newbury that I had nothing further to say to them they followed me back to my home at Lambourn and refused to go away until I had spoken to them again. Fortunately Charles and Carolyn Benson were staying for the weekend because Charles being a journalist himself knew exactly what they were up to. When I told the two men they could print whatever they liked Charles told me that I was wrong. He said that apart from the meal they would make of what they thought I had done it was the principle of the thing and people shouldn't be allowed to break into houses and tap 'phones whenever they felt like it. Until then Miriam and I hadn't even thought how the tapping had actually been done but, when we did, Miriam remembered a night back in November when the

Governor and Oliver Sherwood had brought us home after a dinner dance at Cheltenham. When we got back the front door was open and we thought that we must have been burgled but we couldn't find anything missing and presumed that whoever had got in had heard us coming and left. The thought of having had someone break into our house disturbed Miriam a lot more than it did me and, as she pointed out, if they had been recording my conversations they must also have been recording hers.

Charles suggested that the first thing I should do was to ring my solicitor Matthew McCloy who is also a friend and seek his advice. Given all the facts Matthew thought that they were planning to go to press with a story on the Monday and drove to London the next day to arrange for an injunction. On the Sunday morning the Governor 'phoned to see how I was and I told him that everything was all right but without mentioning anything to Miriam I had started to have my doubts. As far as I was concerned I hadn't done anything wrong but suddenly people were talking about injunctions and barristers and such like. It all seemed unreal. The relaxing weekend that I had planned turned out to be the complete opposite as the 'phone rang constantly with reporters from other newspapers wanting to know what was happening and then messages from Matthew keeping me informed as to his progress. By 5 o'clock he had obtained the injunction and had been told that the case would be heard in court the following Thursday.

He then arranged for Tom Shields and Richard Hartley, who is a QC, to act for us because the *Mirror* had immediately opposed the injunction. I couldn't go to court myself as I was riding at Stratford but Miriam went instead. She wasn't required to say anything but I wanted her to go so that she could keep me informed as to exactly what happened. For her it was quite a traumatic experience and during the five days that the case was being heard she hardly ate a thing and lost quite a bit of weight. On the first day after hearing our evidence the judge found in our favour. He

125

upheld the injunction and ordered that the following day the *Mirror* should disclose who had tapped our 'phone. When I got back from Stratford and heard this I was delighted because by this time I had become extremely curious as to who had done it. The next day the *Mirror* appealed to the Court of Appeal against the injunction but, again, it was turned down. However, the new judges revoked the order for them to disclose their source of information by saying that although they were sympathetic to the fact that our 'phone had been tapped, they also had to take into account the journalistic rights of secrecy. The *Mirror* then successfully argued that they hadn't been given enough time to prepare their appeal and another hearing was arranged for 13 March, which was the first day of the Festival Meeting.

For the Court of Appeal the *Mirror* had engaged one of the best QCs in the country. Matthew told us that, if the new judges went against us and I had to pay their costs as well as my own, I was going to be getting a bill for over £20,000. I could hardly believe it. Somebody had broken into my house and tapped my telephone and I was in danger of facing an enormous bill. Once I realised this I was much more concerned as to the outcome and I made Miriam 'phone me at the racecourse immediately anything new happened.

After three days, in which the balance swung first one way and then the other, the judges finally came down in our favour. They ordered that all the tapes should be handed over and kept in safety by a third party but, more importantly, they awarded most of our costs against the *Mirror*. The report of the case in both the *Daily Mirror* and the *Sporting Life*, which is part of the Mirror Group, seemed biased to me to say the least and one could easily have been forgiven for thinking that it was I who was being taken to court. Once the hearing was over I was determined to sue the *Mirror* for damages because of the worry they had caused Miriam and because I also wanted to know who had broken into my home. The thought that somebody at the *Mirror* actually knew who had done it, and yet wasn't forced to

126

reveal who, makes a mockery of English law and it irritated me.

After a long meeting in London with my barrister he persuaded me that I was dealing with such a grey area of the law that nobody could be certain as to the outcome and that, if the case went against me, I could easily be landed with a bill for £100,000 or more. The risk wasn't worth taking and so the case was left as stalemate. The *Mirror* didn't get their story and I never got the satisfaction of knowing who had broken into my home.

CHAPTER TEN

Being a top jockey may appear to be a very glamorous life but behind the TV interviews and successes lies a lot of hard work. By the end of a normal day when I might have ridden anything up to sixteen horses and jumped may be one hundred and forty fences, I was whacked. The only thing that could persuade me to go out for an evening during the week was if a favourite group of mine was playing somewhere. Just to go to a good pop concert gives me a bigger buzz than anything I ever did riding and I think that if I was given a choice of things I would most like to do it would be to play in a band. On top of the physical effort of riding and the mental strain of organising rides, looking through the form book and arranging to school horses for different trainers, there was then the driving. Unfortunately I have always been prone to car sickness and so although I didn't always take my own car I preferred to do the driving. I used to clock up about a thousand miles a week on average during the season and when I was on my own tended to get bored. However, when there were three or four of us going together we used to have much more fun.

Mooning at coach loads of people on the motorways was always good for a laugh and so was pretending to be policemen in an unmarked car. We would wait until we got behind someone who was speeding and then, all put on our policemen's hats which one of the lads had nicked from a local theatrical shop. Whoever was driving then pulled alongside the offender and blew the horn while the jockey in the passenger seat kept a deadpan expression and signalled for them to pull over. Everything we did revolved around things that made us laugh whether it was through looking at people's faces who thought that they had been caught for speeding or whatever. Roy Mangan's favourite trick when he had a runny nose which seemed to be always was to wait until one of the jockey's fell asleep and then trickle snot over their eyelids so that when they woke up they had to struggle to open their eyes. Watch somebody waking up from a deep sleep who suddenly thinks he has gone blind is far funnier than it sounds and has to be seen to be appreciated.

There is also quite a lot of laughter to be got from frightening people and playing Russian roulette while doing 70 mph over the crossroads near Membury Service Station without looking was as good a way as any. I remember doing something almost as stupid after a trip to Devon and Exeter. Nicky Henderson, Colin Brown, Philip Blacker and I had all gone racing together in the little white Fiat which I had at the time. I had driven all of the way there and then ridden in six races while the others had only two or three rides each. On the way home we had just got on to the M4 at Bristol when I began to feel tired and, when I asked which one of them would like to take over the driving, they all declined, which I thought was unfair considering I'd been doing most of the work all day. I said 'Right then, none of you wants to drive and neither do I.' With that I pulled over the lever which operated the speed control and climbed into the back with Phil and Colin leaving us all going along doing 70 mph with no driver. Nicky suddenly decided he wanted to drive after all and scrambled behind the wheel just in time to alter the course the car had taken towards one of the break-down telephone boxes.

It all seems totally silly now but at the time it caused excitement which is what we thrived on. Steve Smith-Eccles and Ian Watkinson were equally mad. They used to play a game driving home to Newmarket from the races whereby the winner was the one who could score the most points from other drivers. I don't remember exactly but I think that the points values were: two for blow of the horn, four for a V sign, six for flashing lights and a maximum of ten for making the driver pull off the road altogether. Ian, who drove much the same way as he rode, usually managed to win by overtaking on double white lines around a blind bend.

Driving the number of miles that I did and often being in a hurry to get to the races on time, it was inevitable that I was occasionally stopped for speeding but the only time I ever lost my licence was for crossing a set of traffic lights while they were on red. It happened while I was on my way to Leicester. It must have been in 1979 because I remember I was still driving the Renault 5 I had bought after I sold my Rover to John Banks. It was a filthy day and never stopped raining from the moment I, Ben de Haan and two other jockeys set off from Lambourn. Just as we got to the Kidlington by pass I heard the fan belt begin to slip and the further we went the worse it got. Each time I pulled away it sounded as though it were ready to snap but as we were already late and I didn't particularly feel like getting soaking wet trying to mend it, we decided to carry on. As we reached Wheddon which is on the main A348 it began to rain even harder and the visibility dropped to about a hundred yards. Just as we approached the traffic lights, which were about two hundred yards inside the speed limit, they began to change from green to red. I didn't want to risk the fan belt breaking by having to stop and then pull away again so I put my foot down on the accelerator and crossed them just as they turned to red. Unfortunately there was a policeman waiting to cross the lights from the other direction. I had only gone about two miles up the road when he stopped me. They always say that it is best to get out of the car when you have been pulled up by a policeman but it was raining so hard I stayed where I was. In the five seconds that it took him to walk up to my car he got drenched and was struggling to hold his hat on in the wind. I wound the window down about an inch so that I let in as little rain as possible and peered up to him. I could tell from the look on his face that he was not happy about getting wet and when he asked me if I realised that I had crossed a set of red traffic lights in Wheddon doing at least 70 mph I

130

thought that a spot of humour might cheer him up. I replied 'Yes, officer, you don't want to hang about when you go through them on red.' I failed. He virtually dragged me from the car into the wet outside and over to his Range Rover where he booked me. After the subsequent court case where everyone except the policeman had laughed at what I had said I was banned from driving and spent three months going to work on a bicycle.

CHAPTER ELEVEN

26 June 1976 may have been the hottest day ever recorded in London but for me it will be remembered as the day I got married. I had first met Miriam when I was an apprentice and she was working as secretary to Patrick Haslam. She had come to Lambourn originally for just three months as Girl Friday to Ken Payne but when he left to train in Yorkshire she stayed behind.

I remember the first time that I took her out we went to see a horror film in Swindon called *Tales from the Crypt* and then bought fish and chips on the way home. She didn't realise it at the time but this was really pushing the boat out as far as I was concerned. Until then most of my girlfriends had to make do with a Coke and a packet of crisps from the Rose and Crown in Ashbury followed by a drive up to the downs on the pretext of looking at the White Horse. This is always a favourite spot of mine because it is miles from anywhere and I found that all the girls I took there would do anything rather than face a long walk home. Pictures and fish and chips was a completely new experience for Miriam who was much more sophisticated than I was and was more accustomed to the theatre followed by dinner in a nice restaurant. I don't know whether she preferred better food or someone else but we only went out together twice more after that and it was the best part of a year before I plucked up enough courage to ask her out again. By that time my taste had gone from crisps to chicken in the basket and then the White Horse Hill but Miriam would have none of it. She was the only girl I ever took there who actually got out of the car and started to walk. It took nearly eighteen months of regular courting before I eventually got her into bed by which time I was determined to marry her if only out of curiosity. It was the best decision that I ever made and after nine years I can put my hand on my heart and say I'd marry her again tomorrow. We are basically very good friends and both enjoy being at home although we each know we can go where we like when we like and with whom we like and neither of us will mind so long as we are enjoying ourselves.

After a honeymoon in Greece where I spent the first five days in bed with sunstroke we came back and moved into the Corrugated Iron Bungalow which Miriam had managed to transform from a bachelor pad to a home. She made it so comfortable that I didn't really want to move but I had already started building a new house and stables in the field below. Once I had finished paying my parents back the money that they had lent me to buy the bungalow I bought the six-acre paddock next door and got planning permission for a training establishment. I had been interested in building things ever since I was a boy and used to help my father and I did most of the work and all of the designing myself. After I had completed the stables and put the shell of the house up I had the chance to buy a large industrial building in the village very cheaply. The opportunity was too good to miss and so I changed my car for a smaller one and delayed moving into the house for another year until I could afford it. During the time I was suspended from riding following the John Banks Enquiry I dismantled the building and re-erected it at home to use as an indoor school. And it's invaluable. Quite a lot of the local trainers use it to get the young horses jumping at the start of the season and we use it almost every day ourselves for breaking in young horses. While I was enjoying the building Miriam was working hard getting the garden going. I can barely tell an oak tree from a lavatory whereas she knows every plant and shrub that we have. Because of this I am only allowed to mow the lawns and dig where she knows there isn't much danger of my mistaking one of her young plants for a weed.

When we did eventually move into the new house it

looked bare. The lovely pieces of furniture which Miriam's parents had given us as a wedding present were lost in the bigger house and it wasn't until Chick Wilson brought us down a removal van full of lovely furniture and pictures that it began to look like a home. Chick was about eighty and had been a music hall entertainer in his younger days and still did very good impressions. He loved going racing but I think that basically he was really quite lonely and it might have been that I always took the time to stop and talk to him. I remember driving him to the station after Cheltenham one day and telling him how we had just moved into the new home and how empty it was. I didn't know it at the time but he had just sold his house in the country and moved into a flat in London. He suggested that rather than pay storage on what he didn't have room for I might as well use it and so that's what I did. When he died a few years later he left all his furniture to me in his Will.

CHAPTER TWELVE

By the end of the 1983/84 season I reckon I had the game just about as well taped as you can get it. I had been laid up for five weeks during October and November with three cracked vertebrae and yet I had still managed to knock in one hundred and thirty-one winners which was the fourth of five consecutive years that I had passed the ton. In my last two seasons I had the advantage of having John Jenkins' stable as a backup to the Governor and in the first eight weeks of my last season he provided me with an incredible thirty-three winners. I began riding for John originally because it gave me the opportunity to chat up his lovely wife Wendy – the winners were just a bonus! I rode John his first winner on Given in 1979 and rode for him then on whenever I could. It was as near to the perfect job that any jockey could ever get. I never once went to Epsom to ride out or school for him. All I did was just turn up at the racecourse and ride. I didn't even have to do that if I didn't want to. If there was ever any horse that I didn't like I just told him so and he'd say: "That's all right, mate, I'll get somebody else." With him everything was easy. He is a really dedicated trainer and yet he doesn't worry about anything. If he has had a bet which he loves to do and it gets beaten there is no long face – he just smiles and says, "Oh well", and looks forward to the next one. The key to his success is that he gets his horses much fitter than anyone else and as a consequence their races do not take so much out of them. Whenever it came to the business end of a race on one of John's horses and I found it couldn't go the pace, it was only ever through lack of ability and never because it hadn't done enough work.

By June 1984 I had broken Stan Mellor's all time record of

1,035 winners and also won the inaugural running of the Rail Freight World Jockey Championship. But the enjoyment of racing was beginning to fade. I was actually riding better than ever and having as many laughs as usual but the job itself was becoming an effort. Perhaps it was because I had done it all and riding no longer held a challenge for me or maybe it was because I realised that a jockey is only as safe as his last ride and I had reached the point where I had more to lose than I had to gain. Whichever it was I knew that I was having to force myself to do things that before I looked forward to. The prospect of going on chasing all over the country trying to stay on top was daunting and so at the start of the 1984/85 season I made up my mind and told the Governor that it would be my last. I suppose I could have gone on for a few more seasons just picking my rides carefully but that wasn't my style. Nobody can hope to be Champion Jockey that way and if I'm not in the game wanting to be best then I would rather not be in it at all.

Helped by the thirty-three winners from John I had a tremendous start to my final season and when Church Warden won at Cheltenham on 9 November I managed to pip Josh Gifford's record by a day for the fastest fifty winners. Come January I was still going well. I had won the Hennessy and the King George on Burrough Hill Lad and was still in with a chance of beating Jonjo's record of one hundred and forty-nine winners in a season. Then the weather began to turn and with it my luck. By the time I had hung up my boots for good on 9 April I had my seventh Championship in the bag but I had struggled to ride one hundred and one winners in order to just pass my annual target of one hundred. Once Cheltenham and Liverpool were over the days couldn't pass quickly enough and, but for a commitment to compete in the second running of the World Jockeys' Championship, I would have retired on 8 April after I had ridden four winners at Huntingdon. It was just one more example of the many ups and downs of racing because the very next day at Chepstow I parted company with The Reject at the open ditch in the straight and as he did so he galloped all over me. I am not superstitious as a rule but I took this as a hint that it was time to pack up and so that's what I did. It is strange to think that I rode the Governor five hundred and seventy-five winners and yet my first and last ride for him ended up with me being unseated.

The most pleasing thing about my last season was seeing the Governor regain the Trainers' Championship. It had been six years since we had been Champions together and it was the perfect way to end.

I deliberately haven't written much about horses ridden and races won because the winners can be found in the Form Book and, with the odd exception, the horses meant little to me. The tremendous feeling sitting astride a powerful chaser as it soars through the air that some jockeys have written about is something I was never aware of. Riding was my job and the horses were just the tools I worked with. That isn't to say I never cared about them because I did and from the moment I got on one in the paddock to when I dismounted from it after a race I thought of nothing else but their welfare. I rode every horse whether good or bad with the thought in the back of my mind of how it would feel if our roles were reversed and liked to imagine that given the choice it would want me to ride it again.

Whichever way I look at it life seems to be a gamble from beginning to end. Even before we are born someone is spinning a wheel for the most important decision of your life to see who your parents will be which will determine your colour and where you are born. Then there are the countless crossroads that you reach at certain stages of your life where decisions have to be made. They may seem trivial at the time and might only take you on a slight detour but others can take you on a different road altogether. I agree you can create a certain amount of your own opportunities but after that there is something else – as with the time I went to hand in my notice and the Governor had gone out. I sometimes wonder what I'd be doing now if he'd been in. I don't know

137

why most things should always seem to have run in my favour but there is no denying that so far they have. I guess I was just one of those people who was born lucky.

STATISTICS

1st Winner	Multigrey	Worcester	17.11.69
1000th Winner	Observe	Worcester	29.2.84
1036th Winner	Don't Touch	Fontwell	28.5.84
1138th and last Winner	Gamblers Cup	Huntingdon	8.4.85

Wins Abroad

Ireland	2
Italy	2
France	2
Sweden	1
America	3
Jersey	2
Germany	1

	Wins for F. T. Winter	Wins outside
Novice Hurdlers	219	215
Novice Chasers	170	157
Handicap Hurdlers	58	98
Handicap Chasers	128	93
	575	563

INDEX

144